EM&LO'S **REC SEX**

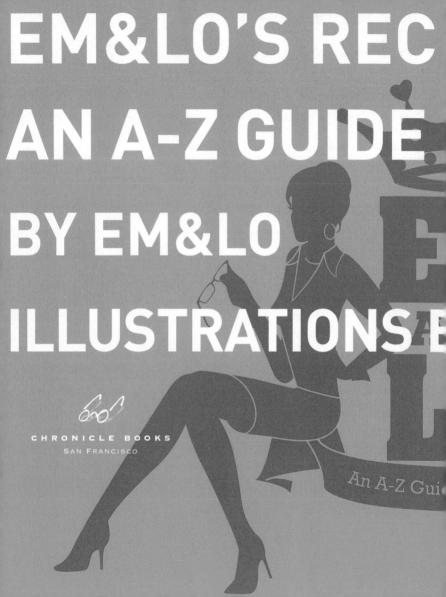

EM&LO'S REC

AN A-Z GUIDE

BY EM&LO

ILLUSTRATIONS B

CHRONICLE BOOKS
SAN FRANCISCO

An A-Z Gui

LIBRARY OF CONGRESS CATALOGING-IN-
PUBLICATION DATA:
TAYLOR, EMMA (EMMA JANE)
EM & LO'S REC SEX : AN A-Z GUIDE TO
HOOKING UP / BY EM & LO.
P. CM.

ISBN-10: 0-8118-5212-1
ISBN-13: 978-0-8118-5212-8

1. SEX—HUMOR. I. TITLE. EM AND LO'S
REC SEX. II. SHARKEY, LORELEI. III. TITLE
PN6231.S54T39 2006
818'.602—DC22

MANUFACTURED IN CANADA

DESIGNED BY AYAKO AKAZAWA
EM&LO LOGO DESIGNED BY
AYAKO AKAZAWA AND DAN SIPPLE

DISTRIBUTED IN CANADA BY
RAINCOAST BOOKS
9050 SHAUGHNESSY STREET
VANCOUVER, BRITISH COLUMBIA V6P 6E5

10 9 8 7 6 5 4 3 2 1

CHRONICLE BOOKS LLC
85 SECOND STREET
SAN FRANCISCO, CALIFORNIA 94105

WWW.CHRONICLEBOOKS.COM

ACKNOWLEDGMENTS

This book would not be possible without all the friends and EmandLo.com readers who constantly give us access to their best (and worst) date scenarios and booty bloopers: in particular, Claire Taitte, Yumi Sasha, and the gang of eighteen at Hannah's Hen Do. Apologies to those friends whose permission was slightly more, shall we say, implicit and who may thus recognize themselves (though no one else will). Thanks also to Rob and Joey for being patient with two advice ladies who can dish it better than they can take it, our parents for continuing to buy our books even if they don't read them, our sisters for always being there, our agent, Ira Silverberg, for being fabulous, and our editor, the amazing Jodi Davis—you had us at "Hello."

INTRO

"Sex is something I really don't understand too hot. You never know where the hell you are. I keep making up these sex rules for myself, and then I break them right away. Last year I made a rule that I was going to quit horsing around with girls that, deep down, gave me a pain in the ass. I broke it, though, the same week I made it—the same *night*, as a matter of fact."–HOLDEN CAULFIELD

Sex is something we understand pretty good, but what you have in your hands here is far from a book of rules. Self-imposed sex rules, it turns out, are entirely useless in figuring out where the hell you are—far better to determine what rules everyone *else* is playing by. (Though, if you're going to follow just one rule, not horsing around with people who give you a pain in the ass is as good as any.) As any navigator worth their compass will tell you, the best way to map your location is to look around you, from the ground beneath your feet to the horizon. And that's exactly what we've done in this encyclopedia—except we looked under the sheets, too.

One of the problems with **casual sex** is that there's a lot more of it going on than there are people who admit to indulging in it. This is in part because all too frequently, only one party considers the sex to be casual (see **unilateral casual sex**). But it's also due to the fact that people personalize their own definitions of casual sex, like so many Trapper Keepers graffitied with Wite-Out.

Maybe "over the shirt, under the bra" before exchanging class rings is classified as a casual **hookup** in your book. Or maybe you don't consider a **one-night stand** to be *truly* casual if you were secretly hoping the person would court you via **Friendster** the following Monday. Perhaps you consider a dalliance to be casual only if you didn't enjoy it. Or maybe you're one of those Park Avenue princesses who thinks nice girls don't *do* casual sex–they merely hook up. (If so, here's a straw so you can suck it up and deal: This book is for you, too.) Others find the term itself problematic–they think *casual* implies that the sex takes no thought and fits as comfortably as your TV-watching comfy pants. But most of us know you have to date for *years* before sex gets like that– hey, there has to be some reward for all the monogamists out there.

Hence, the title *Rec Sex*–a nicer umbrella term for all the naughty things you do. (Plus, it's fun to say.) Rec sex, or recreational sex, is fucking for the fun of it–and, really, if you're not having fun, you're missing the point. That said, rec sex doesn't have a money-back guarantee on a good time for all, nor is it necessarily consequence free. No, rec sex is simply sex between two or more consenting adults, outside of a long-term relationship, with none of the murky connotations of so-called casual sex.

Put it this way: If you're not sleeping exclusively with your soul mate, this book is talking about you. And even if you *are* sleeping exclusively with your soul mate, that doesn't mean you didn't have rec sex before (see **BUT**, or **bi-curious until thirty**), you won't have it again in the future (see **heartbreak sex**), or you're not having it right now on the sly (see **adultery**–and be ashamed of yourself).

Think of this book as a Choose Your Own Adventure: Most entries– and many terms in this introduction–lead to at least two more, via the bolded text. For instance, if you flip to the definition for **one-night**

stand, that will take you to **prenook**, which leads to **sexpectations** and on to **retrosexuals** or **condoms**, both of which will end up at **play party**, if you try hard enough (though probably not without a stop off at **wingman** or **wingwoman**). Which is like six degrees of separation, or six degrees of Kevin Bacon, or **sex degrees of separation**, which, as you can see, is also defined here!

The circular navigation system is no mistake, because when it comes to casual sex—or rec sex, or hooking up, or whatever you want to call all this precommitment rutting—there is rarely a tidy beginning, middle, and end. In fact, sometimes there's none of the three. In the age of **Google**, when there is no such thing as an unanswered or unanswerable question, we can still find ourselves unclear on whether we're **dating** the person we're fucking.

This is an uncharted hookup culture—but, fortunately, we've been taking notes. Voilà—your field guide to fucking, and all that goes along with it: the heartache, the jealousy, the awkward brunches, the unreturned phone calls, the bloopers, the bad pickup lines, the hangovers, the STDs, the earnest attempts to stave off soul-sucking loneliness by simply connecting with another human being, and, oh, yeah, the ridiculous orgasm faces.

about last night

❶ Classic eighties movie (read: big hair, bad dialogue) starring Demi Moore and Rob Lowe as a couple whose **one-night stand** blossoms into a beautiful relationship simply because they themselves are so beautiful. ❷ A follow-up conversation to the previous night's (perhaps misguided) union that's meant to tie up loose ends, either because you're afraid the person misunderstood your casual intentions, or because *you'd* like to pull a Demi-Rob, or because you have abutting cubicles and want to avoid a sexual harassment suit. In the last instance, a lighthearted email—subject heading "about last night," of course—is obligatory.

adultery

One of the naughtier sins outlined in the Ten Commandments (though less harmful to the waistline than gluttony), this is on-the-sly sexual relations with someone other than your committed partner. The term implies egregious lying and usually applies to a *married* cheater, though the poor girlfriend or boyfriend being **cuckolded** would probably beg to differ. "Adultery: two thumbs way down!" —Em & Lo

AdultFriend Finder.com

"The world's largest sex and swingers personals site," according to its tagline. Members go by endearing usernames such as analfreak3, lickerassnow, and pounditforawhile, and they post up-close-and-personal photos of their **assholes**. See also **online personals, Internet**.

Alfie

Classic Michael Caine (and later Jude Law) **lady-killer** role. Memorable line: "I don't want no bird's respect—I wouldn't know what to do with it." When Alfie finally decides to settle down, he's rejected for a younger man. Now, *that's* what it's all about, Alfie.

all-play

A term describing a **group sex** situation (anything from a **three-way** to a motelful) where bench warming is strongly discouraged and all attendees must participate in some way. (Restocking the chips and dip does not count.)

anal sex

How Catholic girls maintain their virgin status. A.k.a. following the letter of the law, not the spirit. See also **loopholing**.

anonymity

❶ Out of town, online, being someone you're not—either because it turns you on or you're afraid of getting caught, or both. ❷ Going to a sales conference in Des Moines and not wearing your Hi! My name is _____" sticker (which may or may not lead to hot, anonymous sex in a hotel room that features soothing, earth-toned art on the walls).

anonymous STD notification

A partner-notification service some STD clinics offer for particularly *active* individuals who have been diagnosed with something—you give them names and addresses, and they send out anonymous "heads-up" letters. Sure, it's pretty weak, but it takes a strong, strong man or woman to rifle through one's **little black book** and make 163 of those awkward phone calls. The clinics figure that anonymous information is better than no information at all. There's even a San Francisco-based Web site that will send out anonymous e-postcards with taglines like "I got screwed while screwing—you might have, too." But we're guessing that the percentage of *legit* postcards going out from sites like this is negligible—the world contains too many bored 14-year-old boys and exes bearing grudges.

appointment sex

A more formalized version of the **booty call**. This kind of sex scheduling is usually done more than 24 hours in advance, when both parties are sober. Email invitations tend to be favored over more casual **text messages** or impromptu phone calls. This kind of arrangement happens more frequently among

the older set—workaholics, recovering alcoholics, single parents, people for whom fart jokes have lost their charm—i.e., those who no longer have the patience (or the liver) to wait until closing time to make a booty call.

arm candy

❶ Someone who is too boring to date, too nice to just fuck, and too hot to waste, so you take them to that art opening/birthday party/work drinks/wedding you're obliged to attend with a date. When you

→

don't try to take them home at the end of the night, you'll simply look like a gentleman/lady. And if you get drunk at the open bar and *do* decide to take them home? Hey, at least it won't be a **coyote ugly** situation. A.k.a. **tofu boyfriend/tofu girlfriend.** ❷ A **gold digger** who trades on their good looks and hot bod for financial security/expensive gifts.

assholes

❶ **Cads**, **roger dodgers**, **players**, **playas**, all our exes. Though they undoubtedly have a certain sex appeal, they are no match for a good-looking **nice guy** (despite conventional wisdom). ❷ Popular orifices to poke during casual sex, as long as you know how to do it safely.

away game

❶ **Casual sex** when you're out of town, especially when you've got a committed partner back home. (Shame on you!) ❷ Sleeping over at someone else's house instead of inviting them back to your place, because you've got a roommate, a live-in lover, or an embarrassing mold problem in your bathroom.

A

B

bachelor party

Pre-wedding party for the groom, traditionally thrown by his male friends to celebrate his upcoming nuptials (or mourn the impending loss of his sexual freedom, depending on how you look at it). These buddies will attempt to re-create the frat parties of their youth, complete with tequila shots and strippers. Many men mistake the bachelor party for a **monogamy** loophole, assuming that an **anonymous** blow job or one last roll in the hay (a.k.a. bachelor party booty) is an unspoken privilege of the soon-to-be-wed, especially if the man's college buddies are paying for it and/or the "one last fling" is wearing nipple tassels. For those in need of a refresher course: Receiving a lap dance is acceptable (though cheesy) bachelor party behavior; receiving a hand job is not— unless, of course, the man's fiancée has given prior, explicit permission. A promise of a promise is still a promise, and a "signed" permission slip that the best man claims to have procured from said fiancée does not count.

bachelorette party

An opportunity for a woman's friends to remind her what a big **slut** she used to be before she got engaged. Condom earrings, fake veils, and fruity shots are common accessories to the evening. The brave man who approaches a thusly accessorized group should expect a round of applause, followed by demands to pose for a (perhaps seminude) photo, give up his boxers to the bride-to-be, and buy a large round of Screaming Orgasms for all partygoers. Drinks delivered, he will be abandoned in the middle of the dance floor with nary a single set of **digits** when the "fireman" stripper shows up to put

→

out the bride-to-be's fire. This Chippendale wannabe will invariably be wider than he is tall, gayer than he is straight, and more hairless than any of the women in attendance. In this case, grooms need not fear any bachelorette party **booty**. However, if the bachelorette entourage travels to a strip club in the Bronx (as seen on HBO's *Real Sex*), where the strippers are very straight, hung like horses, and sexually active right on stage, be afraid . . . be *very* afraid. See also **ladies' night**.

back rub

A sensual massage that leads to sex 90 percent of the time it is administered (if you believe the hype). Usually conferred by a person who's hoping to get lucky with someone they have not gotten lucky with before.

baggage

The set of issues developed from previous, dysfunctional relationships a person brings to a new relationship. They're usually either family related ("My mama didn't love me enough, so now I treat *all* women like shit") or ex related ("My boyfriend cheated on me with my best friend, so I *will* check up on you by reading your private emails"). Though baggage is an expected inevitability in **LTRs** (who doesn't have at least a small carry-on item?), it is typically unwelcome during casual encounters or early in the **dating** cycle. If yours is oversize, consider unloading it during weekly hang sessions with friends or a shrink.

bar

The most popular place to pick up someone for cheap, meaningless, sloppy sex (or, at the very least, a cheap, meaningless, sloppy make-out **sesh** in a dark corner) due to the increased libido and lowered standards of the picker-upper and/or the picker-upee after one too many Cosmos or shots of JD. Should a bar **hookup** fortuitously turn into a lifelong love affair, it won't make for a great meet-cute story to tell the grand-kids—but if you're 83 and still in love, who the hell cares? See also **booze, beer goggles, coyote ugly, romance**.

bartender

Invaluable accomplice in the field of casual sex: They serve up your social lubricant of choice, can help you "send a drink" with finesse, and will chat with you if you get stood up. A friendly bartender who knows your name (or at least your order) may well impress a potential **hookup**. Warning: Multiple bartenders who know your name and your order at establishments across town may throw up a *Leaving Las Vegas* red flag. A flirtatious bartender who is willing to be your **wingman** or **wingwoman** may increase your sexual cur-rency further, especially if they allow you to dis them in favor of your hot prospect. Bartenders themselves are almost impos-sible to pick up due to the intense competition from your fellow patrons, inspired by the **bartender boost**. Of course, if you do manage to beat the odds, a bartender makes an *ideal* **booty call** partner (see

also **fringe benefits**): They'll get you free drinks, they get off just in time to get *you* off, and their work schedule prevents you from scheduling actual dates with them (thereby preventing the two of you from muddying the booty waters).

cises include a glazing over of the eyes or a far-away look, a sudden change of movement or a deliberate slowing down of pelvic thrusting, and/or incoherent mumbling of letters of the alphabet in random order, such as "RBI" or "ERA."

bartender boost

The illusion that anyone standing behind a **bar** and serving alcohol is taller, hotter, smarter, and funnier than they would be if they were serving you a latte. A.k.a. bartender's lift, raising the bartender, bartendency. See also **bartender**.

baseball stats

Something sports guys think about in order to avoid ejaculating—in particular, to avoid ejaculating prematurely. Telltale signs that he's engaging in such mind-over-matter exer-

bases (first, second, third, home)

An old-fashioned metaphor for various states of the heterosexual, one-on-one embrace, usually among young people so obsessed with growing up before their time and "keeping score" that they employ reductive sports analogies. Early on in its inception, first base represented tongue kissing, second base was code for the touching of tatas (hers), third was fondling below the braided belt (his or hers), and getting to home plate, or going "all the way," meant sexual intercourse. **Oral sex** wasn't even part of the equation, since such an intimate act was typically reserved

→

for later in the relationship, *after* penetration. During the eighties and nineties, however, oral sex began to be included in the possibilities of third base. Today, thanks in large part to President Clinton for defining BJs as "not sex," sucking dick has made itself comfortable at second base. Meanwhile, cunnilingus is still largely missing from the playing field because 13-year-old girls with low self-esteem think *giving* head will make them popular, while *receiving* it will make them **sluts**. (Besides, vaginas are ga-ross!) But, hey, at least baseball itself remains a wholesome game, unsullied by corruption, greed, racist players, bad management, or steroid use.

bear market

A **bar**, party, or other mingling spot with unfavorable pickup conditions, such as a kicked keg, a psycho ex in the house, an unfavorable M-to-F (or gay-to-straight, bear-to-fairy, etc.) ratio, too many frat boys/sorority girls, too many skinny boys in ironic tees/chicks in Converse sneakers, too many nauseatingly loved-up couples parroting Woody Allen dialogue, bad lighting, or someone suggesting charades. See also **bull market**.

beard

❶ A partner whose main purpose is to give the public impression that you are heterosexual, when in fact, privately, you're gayer than a Joan Crawford impersonator conference in Vegas. Much more common before the gay rights movement of the seventies and eighties, beards are employed today only by self-hating, closeted, outwardly homophobic, religious zealots living in states between New York and California. ❷ A good friend who pretends to be your partner so as to ward off an unsavory admirer. Often, this is just an excuse to get closer, in a romantic sense, to said good friend. (Pretty sneaky, sis!)

beer goggles

Overestimating how attractive someone is due to the amount of **booze** in your system, otherwise known as being in college . . . oh, let's be honest: otherwise known as being single in your twenties and thirties. The more generous spirited like to think of this phenomenon as proof that alcohol, like death, is the great equalizer. The rest of us will be there with our camera phones to capture the incriminating evidence. A.k.a. booty alcohol level, Cosmo-tinted glasses. See also **coyote ugly**, **last wo/man on Earth**, **last call**.

benched

The state of being put on the back burner indefinitely by a casual sex partner while they decide a) whether to get serious about another partner in their **rotation** or b) whether you're a good enough lay to bother with. A.k.a. on hold. See also **rain check**.

between boyfriends/ between girlfriends

A euphemism for one's pathetic state of singlehood, this phrase tries—and fails—to mask one's debilitating loneliness. As in "I'm between boyfriends right now," suggesting that one is single by choice, man, *by choice.* The term is often overheard at family, high school, or college reunions, and used especially by singles with friends/parents/colleagues who are overly inquisitive, condescending, or prone to matchmaking. For maximum believability, the phrase should be uttered with an air of exhaustion that implies one simply doesn't have the time, mental space, interest in commitment, clean underwear, or focus to *deal* with a relationship right now.

bi-curious

The sexual orientation of every college girl, at least on the dance floor. Unlike **LUGs (lesbians until graduation)**, these bi-triers' primary motivation is the group of Sigma Chis cheering them on from the taproom. In rare cases, this curiosity about the sex one is not instinctually attracted to is acted on by gay people just for the novelty of it, or by straight men who write poetry. See also **BUT (bi-curious until thirty), kissing bandit**.

binge fucking

The casual sex equivalent of carb loading, binge fucking typically happens right before an occasion with an unfavorable booty forecast—e.g., a lengthy family reunion, business travel to a third world country or Idaho, extensive plastic surgery, med school, etc. If you do it right before dumping someone, because you're not sure when you'll next have sex, it is more properly referred to as "being a total dickwad." A.k.a. carnal loading, storing nuts.

[blank] dick

The inability to rise to the occasion of sex as a result of [fill in the blank]. Examples include beer dick, whiskey dick, coke dick, X dick, and crystal dick. Shakespeare said it best, via the porter in *Macbeth*: "Lechery, sir, it provokes, and unprovokes; it provokes the desire, but it takes away the performance: Therefore, much drink may be said to be an equivocator with lechery; it makes him, and it mars him; it sets him on, and it takes him off; it persuades him, and disheartens him; makes him stand to, and not stand to; in conclusion, equivocates him in a sleep, and, giving him the lie, leaves him." That's where Viagra comes in—and, indeed, many club kids toss a little blue pill into their weekend drug cocktail. Ah, the miracles of modern science.

blogging

The twenty-first-century phenomenon that saw everyone with DSL publishing self-indulgent diaries on their own personal Web sites as a sort of poor man's insta-therapy. A blog may include any or all of the following: poor spelling, gratuitous sexual minutiae, links to other blogs, rants about exes, rants about the weather, gushing over a new crush, "photos of me," shout-outs to regular readers, links to "the funniest video clip EVER," photos of naked celebrities, more sexual minutiae, a blow-by-blow of last night's date, photos of celebrities without makeup, "a photo of my new tattoo," the grape-stomping idiot, "more photos of me." For a particularly dubious example, visit StephanieKlein.blogs.com.

blue balls

A lame excuse straight guys use to pressure girls into sex. Yeah, it's uncomfortable. So what? Go home and jack off, you big baby.

body count

The total number of individuals with whom someone has slept. See also **stats, loopholing**.

body-fluid monogamy

The practice of having unprotected sex—i.e., sharing body fluids—with only one other person while using protection or having **outercourse** with all other partners. Popular with the **polyamory** crowd. If there are more than two primaries in a polyamorous relationship who share bodily fluids but are "safe" with all others, it's known as "pooling risks."

Bond, James Bond

❶ The übercharming British spy from the endless chain of far-fetched action movies (based on a series of novels by Ian Fleming) who gets *so* much →

no-strings-attached sex that, had he existed in real life, his dick would have fallen off from some incurable **STD** long ago. ❷ Any British guy who gets pussy galore. A.k.a. 007.

bondage

The consensual practice of using anything from a silk scarf to nylon rope as a restraint during a sexual scenario. Or, better put: something that should never be attempted with a **one-night stand**, a psycho ex, or an ax murderer. And, while we're at it, don't stare into the sun, don't run with scissors, and don't stick your dick anywhere it might get stuck. See also **handcuffs**.

booty

❶ Ass, anatomically speaking (as in "Shake your booty!" or "Shakin' that ass") and sexually speaking (as in "Gettin' some booty tonight" or "Gettin' a piece of ass," meaning *any* kind of sexual **hookup** of some consequence). ❷ A pirate's treasure. ❸ An ass pirate's treasure.

booty break

❶ Temporary period of celibacy. ❷ Reducing the frequency with which you call/see someone in order to steer the relationship toward **booty call** territory and away from the realm of serious **dating**.

booty budge

Short for "booty budget": all the money you *don't* spend on cozy-couple trips to Pottery Barn or Crate & Barrel on a Sunday afternoon. This cash mysteriously disappears while in the

active pursuit of booty, despite your halfhearted attempts to invest it in a Roth IRA (or at least in a Tempur-Pedic bed). You fritter it away on drinks, dinners out, and new clothes from H&M, because you're living in the moment for yourself, rather than thinking long-term with someone else in mind. See also **booty tax**.

booty bump

A hit of a drug, such as crystal meth, taken rectally, usually as a prelude to high-risk casual sex—i.e., condomless sex with a stranger after you haven't eaten or slept in four days. Yay, **HIV**!

booty buzz

❶ The intoxicating freedom of reinventing yourself sexually while on a **one-night stand**. To be extra dirty or to try something new—in other words, to potentially make an ass of yourself—because your **flavor** of the month has no **sexpectations** of you and will probably never see you again. A.k.a. sexophrenia. ❷ The liberating feeling of lowered inhibitions you get from alcohol or drugs, an adrenaline rush (e.g., riding a roller coaster or jumping out of an airplane), or a Betty Dodson workshop. ❸ The heady thrill of finally getting some action after a particularly long dry spell (whether it lasted 2 years or 2 days). A.k.a. hookup high.

booty call

❶ A phone call or **text message** made after 11 P.M. to someone you'd like to have sex with that night, usually because there are no better prospects and/or you've been drinking. Though one would normally make a booty call to a **fuck buddy** or a **friend with benefits**, you may booty call (*verb*) someone you have a potential future relationship with. For instance, say you've been on four dates, you've slept together once, and you're looking forward to seeing each other again this coming Monday, but after a Saturday night out with friends, you grow impatient (and horny) and text message them in the hopes that they, too, are itching to see you before the start of the week. ❷ An impromptu late-night in-person request for **booty**. For instance, you show up on someone's doorstep shitfaced at 3 A.M., slurring "Yo, I was juss in the neighbahoooo . . . ." Or you take a detour on your way home past your local **bar** in the hopes that you'll run into the person you wouldn't mind having sex with right now. A.k.a. booty drive-by. ❸ Your friend with benefits, fuck buddy, or someone you don't even necessarily like but with whom you nevertheless enjoy commitment-free sex.

booty tax

The hidden costs of **casual sex**, financial and otherwise: a) money spent on drinks, dinners out, new clothes from Forever 21 (see **booty budge**), b) unrecoverable lost property (earrings, pagers, underwear, etc.), c) Sunday-night blues, d) Tuesday-morning hangovers, e) the increased risk of **STDs**, f) the mortal fear that you'll never find the One and will end up dying alone with fifteen cats.

bootylicious

❶ Sexually attractive—i.e., totally do-able. ❷ Possessing a voluptuous and curvaceous derriere. ❸ Title of a Destiny's Child song, which goes something like this: "I don't think you ready for this jelly / I don't think you ready for this / Cause my body too bootylicious for ya babe."

booze

The social lubricant responsible for most **casual sex**. Like pairing food with wine, each kind of **hookup** is suited to a particular kind of alcohol: wine for romantic "lovemaking," scotch →

on the rocks for business-trip booty, Sex on the Beach-type drinks with little umbrellas for sex on the beach while on vacation in the Bahamas, anything in a martini glass for an "appointment" with a high-end escort or a particularly well-appointed **fuck buddy**, Milwaukee's Best (a.k.a. "the Beast") for losing your virginity in the woods behind the high school, PBR for hipster hookups in East Village dive **bars**, Jack Daniel's straight out of the bottle for groupie sex, Jaeger shots for date rape.

bounce

❶ A **booty call** that weathers a long-term relationship on your part—i.e., a booty call that is suspended for the duration of your **LTR** and resurrected 6, 9, or even 18 months later. As in, "S/he's got bounce." See also **rain check**, **benched**. ❷ A second definition, in vogue with the kids these days (though not endorsed by this encyclopedia), likens the person you're **dating** to a ball you're about to drop. As in, "Why don't you just bounce?" Please, that's *so* junior high. ❸ How to tell real boobies from fake-ums.

boyfriend material

The favorable qualities a man possesses—stability, success, sense of humor, and bank balance (if she's a superficial beeyotch)—that make him a good candidate for a long-term commitment, if she has anything to do with it, thus making her withhold sex from him for as long as possible. See also **girlfriend material**.

boy toy

❶ The term for a ferociously and unapologetically sexy, low-maintenance, in-demand female whom men want to—and usually can—play with. Made famous by Madonna's chrome belt buckle labeled with the

→

phrase. ❷ A modern flip of the previous definition, referring to a male partner whose appeal is primarily physical, whose age is probably scandalous, and whose accent is possibly European. In other words, the new plastic surgery: You're only as old as the man you feel. A.k.a. toy boy, or **arm candy**. A dubious case could be made that *both* definitions 1 and 2 are feminist. ❸ A young, über-cute gay man, usually in short shorts and shirtless, who either is, looks like, or wishes he were a backup dancer for Britney Spears.

bread-crumb trail

A record of **text messages** and phone calls on your Nokia, pictures on your digital camera, notes on your Blackberry, receipts and matchbooks in your pocket, and anything else that might help you remember how you woke up naked next to this drooling stranger.

breakup sex

One-last-time relations with someone immediately after dumping them or being dumped by them. If you're the dumper, you indulge because it could be a while before you get any again (plus, it just seems like bad manners to turn down the dumpee's request for a roll in the hay for old time's sake after breaking their heart). If you're the dumpee, your goal is to provide such hot sex as to make your new ex regret the decision to dump you in the first place. A.k.a. one for the road. See also **comfort sex**, **grief therapy**, **mercy fuck**.

brunch

An early litmus test for the kind of relationship you'll end up having with a new **casual sex** partner: indulging in a leisurely, sit-down brunch in public usually bodes well for a future committed relationship, sharing a postcoital cup of

→

coffee and a slice of toast usually indicates at least a few more amicable **booty calls** over the next several weeks or months, and skipping breakfast entirely means you'll never see them again. Of course, this system is as accurate as a psychic reading of your future discerned from the pattern of scrambled eggs on your plate: while an early early-morning hour of shared flapjacks may mean neither of you were wearing **beer goggles** the previous evening, it could also mean you're both still too drunk to take them off.

brunch story

Last night's saucy encounter that was good enough to share with friends over eggs Benedict, but too casual to warrant skipping said breakfast with your friends and staying in bed to do the *Sunday Times* crossword with your new partner.

Buffett, Jimmy

The singer/songwriter responsible for the casual sex anthem, "Why Don't We Get Drunk and Screw"—a staple of mega-**bar** chains throughout Florida, played on heavy rotation during spring break. Buffett's song was a precursor to such casual sex classics as Ice-T's "Let's Get Butt Naked and Fuck," Nelly's "Hot in Herre," Kelis's "Milkshake," and, oh, pretty much anything released after the mid-nineties except country or folk. As for Julio (father of Enrique) Iglesias and Willie Nelson's **booty**-ballad duet, "To All the Girls I've Loved Before," excuse us while we yack into our **handbags**.

bull market

A **bar**, party, or other mingling spot with very favorable pickup conditions, such as an open bar, an open patio during the first warm day of spring, a favorable M-to-F (or gay-to-straight, bear-to-fairy, etc.) ratio, just enough skinny boys in ironic tees/chicks in Converse sneakers, flattering lighting, or someone suggesting spin the bottle or pass the orange. See also **bear market**.

great last night," or "Sorry about your cat." See also **Post-it note**.

Joe Schmoe
Accountant by Day
Love Machine by Night

oralskills@hotmail.com
(555) CALL-ME

business card

The wallet-size calling card featuring one's name, phone number, place of business, etc., given out to potential partners in business and/or pleasure as a means of getting in touch later. (Get it? In *touch*?) May also be left on the nightstand when one sneaks out of a new partner's bed at 6 a.m., but only if one scrawls an ironic or self-deprecating billet-doux on the reverse side—e.g. "You were

BUT (bi-curious until thirty)

A post-college lifestyle brought on by extenuating circumstances—one's location, occupation, or hobbies—which extends the usual period of **bi-curiosity**. Geographical influences include hipster communities in urban centers—e.g., the East Village, Williamsburg (Brooklyn), **CAKE parties**,

→

Austin's South by Southwest festival, all of San Francisco. Occupational categories include starving artists, musicians, actors-slash-**bartenders**. Hobbies amenable to bi-curiosity include raves, cocaine, and spoken-word poetry. A.k.a. party bisexual.

buyer's remorse

❶ Waking up after a casual encounter and not liking what you see lying next to you. See also **coyote ugly**. ❷ Waking up one morning after 10 years of marriage and not liking what you see lying next to you. See also **free milk**.

C

cable TV

The only place on the TV dial where people have consequence-free **casual sex**. On the networks, as in real life, there's *always* a price to pay.

cad

❶ A man who is morally reprehensible, unprincipled, dishonorable—you know, the kind of guy who takes naked pictures of you while you're sleeping and posts them on the **Internet**, or who breaks up with you to start **dating** your mom, or who tells you he loves you just so you'll agree to condom-less sex, even though he's got a genital wart sprouting on his frenulum. You know, the kind of guy who is absolutely irresistible and so very, very sexy. See also **assholes**. ❷ Rick Marin, author of *Cad: Confessions of a Toxic Bachelor*, whose author photo would seem to belie the book's contents. Ladies, what *were* you thinking?

cadette

A female **cad**. Now that women have equal rights (even though they make only seventy-five cents on the dollar) and they hold positions of power (even though only two Fortune 500 companies have female CEOs) and they are their own sexual agents (even though rape and domestic violence are still epidemic) and they are thoroughly independent (though many still must "graciously submit to the authority of their husbands"), women these days, drunk with all this power, can fuck just like cads: selfishly, irresponsibly, and without consideration or kindness. The *only* recorded example of this phenomenon, however, is Demi Moore playing a corporate cadette in *Disclosure*.

CAKE parties

"Sex-positive," "female-centric" themed dance parties in New York City and London featuring lap dancers, lingerie, and hipster porn, a.k.a. the biggest make-out **sesh** you've ever seen. Yay, oral **herpes**! CAKE membership is just for women; men may attend events by invite only. Photo galleries of these parties show sexually confident women of every shape, race, and orientation thoroughly enjoying themselves in various states of undress while the men, simultaneously dumfounded and giddy, try to insert themselves into the melee in their skivvies. Visit www.cakenyc.com.

caller ID

One of those technological advancements you don't know how you ever lived without, like **TiVo** or nipple clamps. Invaluable to **playas**, this device allows you to answer when your crush calls, return the call later if you're playing hard to get, or banish to voice-mail such undesirables as a clingy **hookup**, a disgruntled ex, your boss, Amex, or your **mom**.

canoodling

What your pre-whoopee face smooshing is called if you're famous enough for it to be noted in the *New York Post*'s Page Six gossip column, as in, "Just asking . . . which Republican Party offspring with a widely rumored substance abuse problem was spotted canoodling a recently wed *O.C.* star at the Lobby Lounge of the Mandarin Oriental last night?"

casual sex

Anything sexual that occurs outside of a **dating** scenario or a long-term relationship, with no *potential* dating scenario or **LTR** in mind. See also **game playing**, **rec sex**, **unilateral casual sex**.

catalyst

Something (or someone) that initiates or accelerates a chemical reaction: décolletage, a pronounced bulge in the jeans, a nosy matchmaking aunt, **booze**, oysters (because placebos count, too), a dirty email, dinner at Nobu, a hot Chinatown masseuse, whispering in one's ear, a sincere compliment, love at first sight, decent porn.

cereal aisle

The best location in a grocery store to assess a good-looking stranger's personality, assuming you're fond of **cruising** the Piggly Wiggly for **booty**. If he's buying Apple Jacks, he's probably single and a bit immature. If he's buying Kashi Go Lean Crunch, he's probably taken. If *she's* buying Apple Jacks, she probably eats three of them off her pinkie finger for breakfast and won't date anyone her miniature poodle doesn't approve of. See also **frozen food aisle**.

cereal sex

A random **one-night stand** in the middle of a sexual/romantic dry spell: It's delicious while it lasts, but it's not filling, and an hour later you're hungrier than you were before you "ate."

cheerleader

❶ An overenthusiastic onlooker at an **orgy**—one who's prone to such outbursts as "Nice money shot!" or "Get your butt up higher!" ❷ A **wingman** or **wingwoman**. ❸ A good costume for a naughty role-playing scenario in the bedroom. ❹ School-sponsored smut for kids.

C

classifieds (*archaic*)

Bite-size personal ads in print. Back in the olden days of ye olde shoppes and shit, people would search for soul mates and/or anal-play partners by placing small, cheap ads in the back pages of local papers and magazines, using a variety of space-saving acronyms like SWF (single white female), ISO (in search of), NSBMWHSSSAHC (nonsmoking black man with Hamptons share, stinky socks, and huge cock)—you get the idea. Classifieds had a bad (albeit justified) reputation for being a last resort for lonely hearts and social outcasts. The advent of the **Internet** and a whole slew of computer-savvy, horny young'uns made searching for soul mates et al. cool (which means it became mainstream and uncool shortly thereafter). So, imagine the dregs of society who continue to resort to the now *ultra*-uncool and outdated, uncreative print classifieds. The horror, the horror . . .

clichés

Stock phrases that have no place in the world of **casual sex** negotiations, unless they are uttered with a healthy dose of hipster irony: "What's your sign?" "**Your place, or mine?**" "**Would you like to come in for a nightcap?**" "**Was it good for you?**" "**When will I see you again?**" Barfaroni! See also **pickup lines**.

closing the deal

❶ Consummating a relationship when you're more concerned with the consummation than the relationship. Typically followed by a mild sense of disappointment, then a dejected browse through one's cell phone address book, and culminating in the creation of a new username on **Nerve Personals**. ❷ The figurative handshake between two people, often during **last call**, that confirms they will have sex together in the immediate future.

C

closure

Sex with an ex to prove to your-self (and perhaps to the ex) that you're finally over them. When it works, it's empowering—and, hey, it's sex! When it doesn't work, it morphs into pathetic **take-me-back sex**. But, hey, at least it's sex!

cock block

The act of preventing a man from scoring. This can be done by the object of affection (OOA) with lame excuses such as "I have to get up early tomorrow" or "My cat misses me." It can be done by friends of the object of affection, who might drag said OOA away for mandatory group dancing to "Toxic." It can be done by a "friend" of the man, either accidentally or with malicious intent, for example by asking, "Are you still dating that girl?" or recounting that funny story about the time the dude's mom found him naked in his room with a bowl of Jell-O. Or it can be done by a jealous competitor, who might frame the man for an unpaid **bar** tab in order to move in on the OOA while the cock-blockee settles his bill. A.k.a. running interference, sexotage.

coffee

❶ Perfect for a blind date if a) you just got out of rehab or b) boozy blind dates cause you to do things you later regret. See also **coyote ugly**. ❷ If the person you're seeing suddenly suggests meeting "for coffee" late in the day and you think, "Jim never has a second cup of coffee," you're probably about to get dumped.

C

collectible

Someone you sleep with because of a certain category or type they fulfill, also known as the "before-I-die" fuck—as in, "Before I die, I would like to have sex with a *Survivor* winner, a former grade-school teacher, one of my old baby-sitters, a **MILF**, a redhead, a truck driver, a politician, some-one outside my own race, a Republican, a goat." Or, "Last night I added a D-list celebrity to my collection." Inspired in part by a character in the cult movie *Last Night* who scrawls his un-PC sexual to-do list on his kitchen wall. See also **doing it for science**, **try-sexual**.

comfort cock

A "blankie" substitute for an adult with attachment issues. For instance, you like to fall asleep holding his manhood, or you wake in the middle of the night to find your hand nestled around it. Assuming he's game, there's nothing inherently wrong with comfort cock—it's certainly a whole lot sexier than actually bringing your mangy blankie to bed. However, the owner of the comfort cock in question may find your clingi-ness a tad disconcerting if, say, you're at the movies on a blind date. See also **comfort sex**.

comfort sex

The sexual equivalent of mac and cheese: sex after a bad day at work, a terrible breakup, a tragic pet death—anything that makes you long for the consol-ing feel of warm skin on skin, of connecting with another soul. It's slow, deliberate, usu-ally missionary, with face hold-ing and perhaps Rachmaninoff playing in the background. A.k.a. a pick-me-up. See also **comfort cock**, **grief therapy**, **mourning period**.

commitment

The state of being bound emotionally, intellectually, and physically to another person with . . . zzzzzzzzzzzzzzzzzzz—sorry, where were we?

commitment-phobe

❶ A man. ❷ A person who's afraid of **commitment**, settling down (or just plain settling), intimacy, **monogamy**, "attached strings," obligations, ultimatums, or anything else that restricts their freedom to fuck without responsibility. This behavior is typically seen in tandem with **Groucho Marx syndrome**. ❸ My ex, the slut—you know who you are.

common-law relationship

The state you and a partner find yourselves in when a **booty call** or casual sleeping/**dating** arrangement survives against all odds (and against your better judgment, perhaps) beyond its typical shelf life. You may not have had the "let's-be-exclusive" conversation, and you may have "hung out" for many months before you saw each other in daylight or while sober, and you may have had the best intentions of just using each other for sex. But, hey, just because you didn't mean to be an item doesn't mean you're not. Wanna double date?

condoms

Barrier protection that you *need to use correctly every time you have casual sex* and there's a penis involved, but that you talk yourself out of using in the

→

heat of the moment, because your judgment is impaired by alcohol, drugs, or lust, because you hate the feel of rubber, because you hate the smell of rubber, because you hate to interrupt the magic, or because your new partner seems like a nice, clean, responsible person. Then, when your doctor diagnoses you with genital warts, you leave the office fighting back tears and ride the subway home all alone in this cold world, convinced that you're a tainted human being who should be ashamed of yourself, that you'll never have sex again, and that no one will ever love you because you're not worthy of love. You'll swear off sex for 6 months to a year, watching **TiVo**'ed USA marathons of *Law and Order SVU* every Friday and Saturday night. Until one day you realize that more than 75 percent of the sexually active population will be exposed to **HPV** (human papillomavirus) at some point in their lives, that it can be managed with regular doctor visits and a healthy lifestyle,

and that condoms significantly reduce the risk of its transmission. Then you *will* use condoms correctly every time you have casual sex (after you've given your partner an HPV heads-up, of course). Why didn't you just listen to us in the first place? Jeez.

conquest

Don't make us dignify this term with a definition. See also **closing the deal**, **roger dodger**.

contraception

Birth control, which includes condoms, the Pill, the Patch, IUDs, diaphragms, cervical caps, spermicidal creams and jellies, vasectomies, tubal ligations, bad **pickup lines**, the Clapper lighting system, and John Tesh compositions.

C

coyote ugly

❶ A degree of hideousness in the partner whom you discover lying beside you after a night of heavy **boozing** that makes you want to chew off your own arm rather than wake him or her in order to make your escape. See also **beer goggles**, **buyer's remorse**.
❷ A lame **bar** in Manhattan where the beer is served in cans, the liquor is served in shots, the jukebox plays trucker music, and the patrons get shitfaced, dance on the bar, and go home with strangers, only to wake up the next day wishing they could gnaw off their own arm in order to make a fast getaway.
❸ A terrible movie about that lame bar.

Craigslist

A noncommercial online community of discussion forums, classifieds, and personal ads founded in 1995 in San Francisco by—wait for it—a guy named Craig. It quickly outgrew its britches, and today there's a Craigslist for almost every major city worldwide, from Boston to Bangalore, from Austin to Auckland. Unarguably the most entertaining section of any Craigslist is the Casual Encounters board, which features posts by an endless array of adorable characters: "Sexy and passable tranny in the Bronx looking for a guy

→

with a big dick for discreet encounter" and "Straight guy looking to watch **glory hole** in action" and "Beautiful 24yo goddess in midtown ISO cleaning slave prepared to be humiliated, cursed at, and hit" and "Orally gifted gentleman with a velvet tongue for your total pleasure" and "Hungry suckmouth for TOTAL top!" and "Adorable, silly, sexy suit" who asks "Wanna smoke a doob & make out?" Oh, and how could we forget "Male toilet ready for use" or the gentleman who will "buy you and use you as I choose"? Whether or not you're interested in anonymous afternoon sex, Craigslist will provide hours of high-quality procrastination, some titillation, and a bit of insight into the darker side of human sexuality. Plus, you might even find an antique lamp for your apartment.

cruising

❶ The act of being in pickup mode in an irony-free zone, such as Idaho, the fifties, LA's Sunset Strip, Miami, or anywhere overrun by spring breakers and *Girls Gone Wild* camera crews. ❷ Trolling for gay male sex. Decades ago, it meant eyeing a hot prospect and following him for fifty city blocks; these days it means a few minutes on **Craigslist**.com, **AdultFriendFinder.com**, or m4m4sex.com, ordering some free take-out sex, and getting delivery within the hour. See also **HIV**, **home game**, **STD ennui**.

cuckold

Archaic term for a man with a straying wife, stemming from the days when this act, as perpetrated by a female, had more to do with disobedience than infidelity—i.e., when "How dare you break my heart?" was usually trumped by "How dare you disrespect *me*, a *man*?"

cuddle party

❶ A nonsexual, judgment-free space to explore touch, intimacy, and affection

with a bunch of strangers while wearing pajamas. It's just like an **orgy**, but without all the drugs and hardcore fucking. Founded by REiD Mihalko (we're not even kidding about that capitalization) and Marcia Baczynski, two sex and relationship coaches, their Flannel Revolution provides people with the affection they enjoyed before seventh grade, when it suddenly became uncool to be touched by anyone other than your girlfriend/boyfriend or your doctor. Yes, it's New Age-y, and, yes, world music *will* be played in the background, but they do have a sense of humor: "The first rule of Cuddle Club: No **dry humping**! The second rule of Cuddle Club: No **dry humping**!" (Hey, it was funny a few years ago.) And don't try to tell us you couldn't use a hug right now: One sincere hair tousle and you'd be reduced

→

→ to a quivering mass of tears, longing to return to the safe and cozy nook of your mommy's neck. Sign up at Cuddleparty.com.
❷ Fully clothed spooning as a result of one half of a new couple holding out, or both partners being too drunk to do anything else.

cybersex

Like phone sex, except over a high-speed **Internet** connection. Remember how, back in the mid-nineties, everyone and their mother (okay, maybe not the mothers) used to meet in chat rooms for one-handed typing sessions, exclaiming their unbridled lust with phrases such as "im rokhard 4 u & want to cum on yr tits!!!" Yeah, neither do we.

D

Daily Show factor, the

A pre-**TiVo** booty benchmark—i.e., is a **casual sex** prospect worth missing *The Daily Show* for? Hey, that show is freakin' hilarious and makes the world seem a saner place, so sometimes it's worth a night or five in.

dancing

❶ Rhythmic gyration to music, either in public at clubs and weddings or in private . . . in front of the bedroom mirror . . . in nothing but underwear. Usually a decent indication of how smooth someone's moves will be sexually, though there are exceptions: Those lacking even a shred of rhythm usually make up for it in oral prowess, and those who surprise the unsuspecting from behind with violent pelvic thrusts on the dance floor usually have teeny dicks. ❷ What women do in a circle around their **handbags** when out on a **ladies' night** or at a **bachelorette party**.

date

An ancient mating ritual that involved the male of the species asking a female whether she would like to "go out sometime." An affirmative response meant that the male would pick her up at her place—say, around seven—and the two would proceed to the malt shop, the bowling alley, or the drive-in. The male would always pay, which meant he felt entitled to stick his tongue down her throat or cop a feel. If both parties could stand each other, more dates would follow until the male gave the female his varsity jacket or school ring, at which point they would be "**going steady**," or he would give her an engagement ring, which would mean they were, um, engaged—in either case it meant he no longer had to pay for things in order to make out with her or touch her boobies. The date was gradually replaced with **hooking up**, a vague and amorphous set of romantic and sexual interactions that defies definition, rule setting, expectations, and old-fashioned gender stereotypes. Once assumed extinct from the romantic world, the date has recently made a comeback with the advent of **online personals**, since online interactions ultimately result in two (or occasionally more) parties setting a date and time in order to meet face-to-face to determine whether they can stand each other. In its new iteration, gender roles are much more fluid: boys may "date" boys, girls may "date" girls, couples may "date" boys or girls, the girl may initiate the "date," either party may pay for the activities of said "date," and the girl may attempt to cop a feel.

dating

More than just sleeping with each other but less than a full-blown, meet-the-parents relationship. People *used* to think that "dating" meant you hadn't shown each other your **assholes** yet, but that was back in the eighties. Some assume that exclusivity is implied by the term *dating*, but unless the words "Let's be exclusive" have been uttered, there's no guarantee. Beyond that, your guess is as good as ours.

deal breaker

Anything that might prevent you from following through on a **one-night stand**, a relationship, a blind date, etc. For instance, they suffer from halitosis, still live with Mother, have a criminal record, smoke, smoke crack, are a first cousin, once dated your best friend, vote for *American Idol* but not for local politicians, listen to Celine Dion, use *gay* to mean "lame" in a junior-high way, or get upset if you use *gay* to mean "lame" in a junior-high way. They're also known as standards, and they're neither watertight nor beerproof. See also **dry run**, **reference check**.

dejafuck

❶ Unexpected sex with someone you weren't planning on seeing or sleeping with again. For instance, after a few keg stands, you spent one of your last college Saturday nights in a room at Kappa Kappa Gamma with what's-her-name, never to see her again, until 10 years later, when you bump into her at the international trade convention in Dallas, and, after a few Maker's Marks at the Hilton, end up in her room for old time's sake. ❷ One of the **Samantha Jones** plotlines on *Sex and the City*: an unwitting **booty** repetition (i.e., you don't realize you've already slept with this person until you catch sight of their third nipple—or, worse, until you see their orgasm face).

designated dialer

A friend who agrees to monitor your cell phone usage and watch for you waxing nostalgic with that misty look in your eyes, which usually precipitates a **drunk dialing**. This friend has your prior, *sober* permission to confiscate any mobile calling devices, should they find your judgment to be seriously impaired. Designated dialers are particularly handy

→

D

→

in the immediate aftermath of a breakup, if you are trying to gain **hand** in a **booty** situation, or if you have no shame.

digits

The hipster term for a telephone number, usually one given to or procured from a prospective sex partner and clumsily scribbled on a cocktail napkin, the back of a **business card**, or a palm. More often than not, the number is never dialed. When it is dialed, it frequently leads to a mattress wholesaler, the It's Just Lunch! dating service, or a heartless message from a phone operator informing you that the number hasn't worked for, like, years. See also **bars**, **faux no.**, **Rejection Hotline**.

dipping your pen in the company inkwell

What employee "relations" are called when crotchety old Arnold from Accounting gets it on with Candy from Customer Service, who spent her holiday bonus on a boob job and is one **Post-it note** short of a full pad. When *you* do it, on the other hand, it's just a matter of convenience **dating**. Around the water cooler, it's called car pooling, as in, "Did you see who car pooled to work again this morning? Heh-heh." While old school-ers frown on this activity, dating in the workplace actually makes sense, if you think about it. **Bars** were made for flirting, not soul mate searching; interview-style online dating takes too much time for a workaholic; and friends and family members cannot be relied on to set you up with the "perfect guy." Considering all this, how can you *not* date a coworker, especially when you

→

spend the majority of your waking hours at the office? It's just practical—and, at least, with a coworker, you already know you like them in daylight. As long as you're not abusing your power by, say, promising an underling a raise (and not just the kind in his pants), or climbing the corporate ladder the "old-fashioned" way, interoffice romances have legitimate perks: taking long lunches at nearby midtown motels, sending saucy instant messages, sneaking off to the supply closet, and doing it after hours on the CEO's desk—while getting paid overtime! Not to mention all the gas you'll conserve by car pooling to work. Fortunately, dipping your pen in the company inkwell (or vice versa) is still taboo enough to make things a little exciting—call it danger lite—but not so taboo that you'll be ostracized from your community or thrown in jail. And if it goes against office policy? Depending on your job satisfaction, getting fired may be a risk

worth taking for love, if not *Disclosure*-style lust. A.k.a. coworker sex, work liaisons.

dirty talk

Stuff that doesn't translate well to print. Some find it easier to dabble in either with a **one-night stand** (as a result of a **booty buzz**) or with a **fuck buddy** (because the relationship is based solely on porno-inspired sex).

dirty weekend

A mini-getaway in which the sole aim is to dirty someone else's sheets (and we don't mean your Aunt Nora's). If the room comes with a water bed, a Jacuzzi, fake wood paneling, or a view of the Vegas strip, you're on a dirty weekend. Engaging in nothing but missionary-position sex, however, automatically demotes your weekend to **vanilla** status. To be safe, be sure to pack more **lube**, **condoms**, and strap-ons than you think you'll need. A.k.a. weekender.

discreet

Code word, usually used in the realm of **online personals**, that loosely translates as "I am a lying, cheating, scheming, selfish person who's promised someone my undying loyalty and **commitment**, but I am willing to turn my back on that for a blow job."

dogging

Sex in a public place, such as a parking lot or a park, usually with an audience, and typically in a car (though a set of wheels is not required). In some cases, audience participation is encouraged. A predominantly British and heterosexual phenomenon, dogging has resulted in a slew of U.K. Web sites dedicated to the where's and the how's—there's even a music video by Urockers, a "collective of sexual anarchists born of the Internet," called "Dogging," which goes something like this: "Sex in public feels so right / Honk your horn / It's a dogger's delight!" U.K. health-protection agencies are up in arms over the **STD** risks and/or the idea that people are having a raucous good time. Depending on whom you believe, the term comes from the meaning "to watch or follow," from the idea of having sex like dogs, or from the word *doggery*, which means "rabble" or "mob." Not to be confused with your local high

→

school's make-out point; there, a knock on the window and a polite "May I join in?" would probably not sit well with the captain of the football team, who's "**parking**" (*not* dogging) with his underage cheerleader girlfriend.

doggy style

Recommended sexual position if you are in the bad habit of accidentally blurting out "I love you!" during **one-night stands**.

I love you!!!

doing it for science

❶ Engaging in a sexual experience not because you're necessarily "into" it, but just because you want to see what it's like. For an example, see **bi-curious**. See also **collectible**, **try-sexual**. ❷ Signing up to be a paid guinea pig in a sex study you saw advertised on the back page of your local alt weekly because you're totally broke. ❸ The Nerve.com column originally written by Grant Stoddard, for which he'd submit himself to various sexual experiences— cross-dressing, plaster casting his penis, becoming an adult baby—and report back with much hilarity for the benefit and edification of his readership.

Donna

Someone who acts as if a roll in the hay with them were season-finale material, à la Donna from *90210*. This is primarily, though not exclusively, a female affliction. A Donna will dangle sex like a carrot, and then expect to be awarded generously once they let you nibble on that carrot, as it were. A Donna, left unchecked, may blossom into a **gold digger**.

do-over

A second chance at a **pickup line**, a **date**, a **kiss**, a sex act, or a relationship that went horribly, horribly wrong the first time. For instance, let's say your adult retainer falls out right as you're leaning in for that oh-so-romantic, we'll-remember-this-moment-forever first kiss. In that instant, it would not be entirely inappropriate to cry out, "Do-over!"

double-headers

When two consecutive sexual congresses with two partners are not punctuated by at least one of the following: sunset, change of location, change of outfit, change of sheets, or change of heart. If the two appointments are not even separated by a shower, it's called shifting on the fly, not to mention just plain gross.

double standard

Let's define by example, shall we? Guys who have a lot of sex are studs, while girls who have a lot of sex are **sluts**. Or, it's funny when guys fart but ghastly when girls pass gas. In other words, total fucking bullshit. See also **glass ceiling**, **reputation**, **virgin-whore complex**, **equal opportunity objectification**.

dress up, to

Wearing something out of character, in *or* out of the bedroom. For women, it is usually akin to embracing their inner **slut**. For men, it may be trying on their girlfriend's lacy underpants (though the fantasy is rarely realized, for fear she'll tell her best friend/sister/therapist/mom/someone likely to speak at their wedding). Which is why casual **hookups** offer the perfect opportunity for dress-up: During **rec sex**, your partner has very little insight as to your actual character (see also **booty buzz**, **sexpectation**), and, thus, you might be the only one in on the fact that your plunging neckline, tighty-whities, or gimp suit actually qualifies as "dress-up" (okay, so your constant fidgeting in the gimp suit might be a bit of a giveaway). See also **Halloween**.

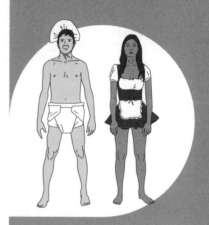

drive-thru

❶ Convenient sex—i.e., you stop by for a quickie and then keep on moving. ("I hate to come and run, but I've got a plane to catch.") ❷ A person who is easy sexually—i.e., they're always "open" for late-night business, just like Wendy's.

drunk dialing

Calling, while under the influence, someone you're having sex with, someone you want to have sex with, or someone you used to have sex with. Especially common after a breakup, near closing time, or when you're shitfaced. Drunk dialing—as opposed to making a **booty call**, which is frequently conducted while tipsy but is not necessarily, or by definition, drunk dialing—implies that one's judgment is impaired and one is making a call that will be regretted in the morning, whether or not the call results in booty. If you drunk dial your buddy just to slur, beer commercial-style, "I love you, man!" it's kinda cute, especially if you're not normally the emoting type. If you drunk dial your **mom**, you should consider therapy. See also **designated dialer**.

D

dry humping

❶ The bumping and grinding of genitals in an attempt to get as close to intercourse as is possible while fully clothed, usually practiced by teens or born-again Christians who are not ready to go all the way. ❷ The bumping and grinding of genitals on the dance floor in an attempt to get as close to intercourse as is possible, usually practiced by meat-heads without the express

→

permission of women, who eventually throw their Red Bull-and-vodkas in the interlopers' faces. See also **dancing**. ❸ Frottage. ❹ What your dog does to your leg. ❺ Something Lo did to the corner of the living room coffee table when she was six.

dry run

Or, more formally, dry-*humping*-run: When you go home with someone but you don't go all the way (for it to really count, you should keep on underwear and a tee). The dry run is in part a fact-finding mission to uncover potential **deal breakers**, though it is also considered a safeguard against a rising **body count** to idiots who keep score like that. Pertinent details that may present themselves during a dry run include an aggressive, awkward kissing

style, a particularly large stuffed-animal collection, black satin sheets, Depend undergarments in the bathroom cabinet (not that we condone looking, of course), two cozily nestling toothbrushes in a studio apartment for one (unless you're there for a **three-way**), a custom-built dungeon (unless that's your bag, baby), one or more framed photographs of Mommy or Daddy *on the nightstand*. A.k.a. the test drive. See also **reference check**, **outercourse**.

Dutch courage

Bravery inspired by liquor. Specifically, the inspiration two shots will give you to interrupt the taping of an episode of *ANTM* at an NYC **bar** in order to ask Tyra Banks to dance, even though there's no music playing—and you're half her height. The idiom

→

comes from the centuries-old notion that the Dutch like to get their buzz on. Have you *been* to Amsterdam? See also **booze**.

dutch, going

❶ Splitting the bill so there's no confusion as to whether sexual favors are expected in exchange for the lobster. ❷ Sex while stoned. ❸ Sex in clogs (*obsolete*).

E

early adopters

Booty trend-setters. They were poking and accepting pinkies in the back door back when *everyone* thought it was gay; they were using the Rabbit Habit vibrator before it was a plot-line on **Sex and the City**; they were the first to figure out that **text messages** were practically invented for **booty calls**; they are the inspiration for this book; they are our hope and our future.

early decision

What one party in a new relationship pushes the other to make in the beginning stages of **dating**, the choices being a) exclusivity (see **commitment** or **monogamy**) or b) breaking up. This push for immediate exclusivity may be made in order to passive-aggressively control and possess the other, to lower the risk of spreading **STDs**, or simply (and romantically) to give the idea of a monogamous relationship a chance—so you'll have a nice, wholesome story to tell the grandkids one day.

economies of scale

A theory of **seduction** (and don't make us say that again) positing that the more you put yourself out there, the better you'll do. *Duh*, you say. But, like the greatest economic theories, it gets better as you unpack it. Say you spy the woman/man of your dreams sipping a green-tea latte at the Soy Luck Club café: You're almost guaranteed to spaz out when you approach them, unless you're naturally blessed with balls/labes of steel. What hope do you have of maintaining your cool as you try to give your future spouse your **digits**, scrawled on an unbleached, recycled napkin?

→

→ What if, instead, you approached every cutie who ever caught your eye, on a daily basis? The stakes would be much lower, because you couldn't possibly go out with every one of them—so what would you care if you got a rejection or two or fifteen? This laissez-faire approach lowers your desperation level, which inversely affects your sex appeal. Now, *that's* what we call a return on investment. Once you've mastered your master-of-seduction role, resist spreading the love too thinly, lest you leave a trail of broken hearts in your wake.

Ecstasy

Club drug notorious for fueling impromptu massages, **cuddle parties**, G-rated **three-ways** and **orgies**, and **drunk dialings** to your sorority sister/fraternity brother.

ego boost

❶ A result of responses to your posting on an **online personals** site, especially when you're nursing a broken heart—even if you're not interested in the respondents, it's nice to know someone, *anyone*, is interested in you. ❷ Sex with someone who's really into you, who tells you everything you want to hear, who compliments your sparkling eyes and soft, sweet-smelling hair and impressive endowments, and whom you will dump faster than a flaming bag of poo as soon as they've made you feel like a more worthwhile person. ❸ Sex with a model, a celebrity (D-listers count), or a luminary in a field you respect (like Pulitzer Prize-winning author Michael Chabon—ooooh, he's dreamy). ❹ A drink sent to you from across the **bar**. ❺ An email to your personal **blog** asking if you'd consider selling your used underwear. ❻ Sex.

E

email

The best medium for dumping someone after two dates, asking out a coworker, following up after a blind date, initiating an **about last night**, making an indecent proposal to a **fuck buddy**, or passing on the Neiman Marcus cookie-recipe hoax. The *worst* medium for dumping someone after 2 years, telling someone you may have given them genital **herpes** (see **anonymous STD notification**), or explaining your fondness for "alternative" water sports (and we're not talking about male synchronized swimming).

emissions, bodily

❶ Any of the following: saliva, drool, pre-ejaculate fluid (or pre-come), semen, come, cum *[sic]*, vaginal secretions or juices, farts, vaginal queefs, anal queefs (a.k.a. the little death sigh), spontaneous

and ill-timed confessions of love. ❷ The *real* stars of the *American Pie* trilogy, Ben Stiller farces, and most gonzo porn. ❸ The little trumpet Em played in her pants while we were writing the entry for **ego boost**.

ennui

An emotional state wherein you, an avowed single, find yourself ogling happy couples at brunch, art galleries, and the Natural History Museum, and either wishing them bodily harm or wishing *you'd* get hit by a bus. Unless you embark on an **LTR** soon, or at least temporarily refrain from casual **hookups**, you may find yourself blurting out inappropriate remarks to your **one-night stands** such as "I love you!" or "Don't leave me!"

EPT

❶ Emergency Pregnancy Test. Not something you should need if you're engaging in casual sex (unless you're *really* unlucky) because the heedful hooker-upper always uses two forms of birth control, i.e. a barrier method such as a condom (for STD protection) *and* the Pill, the Sponge, etc. ❷ Emergency Pubic Trim. Typically performed just before closing time with a pair of nail scissors in a bar bathroom, or with a borrowed razor in your one-night stand's bathroom where you excused yourself for a moment before **closing the deal**. Common after a long dry spell, an EPT is entirely unnecessary in our book—only a hair nazi would turn you down at this point, and you'd actually be doing the more hirsute hooker-uppers of this world a favor by spreading a little tolerance for diversity down there. But hey, if that's what it takes for you to lie back and lose yourself in some mindblowingly fabulous, anonymous rimming or oral lovin', then don't let us stop you. See also **play d'oh!**

equal opportunity objectification

When women get in on the ogling game. Okay, we *get* it: Men are visual creatures. But chicks like to look, too! Maybe not so much that we're willing to start wars for a peek below the belt (like Paris of Troy did over Helen), but give us a chance: Centuries of patriarchal repression haven't exactly encouraged us to be our own sexual agents, nor have they given us many aesthetically pleasing images of heartthrobs (emphasis on the *throb*) to appreciate sexually. Michelangelo's David is a grower, not a shower, and *Playgirl* is for gay guys. Is it too much to ask that for every gratuitous tit shot, we get a

→

butt shot? Or how about some full frontal male nudity for a change? Harvey Keitel, Ewan McGregor, and Kevin Bacon can't bear the burden all by themselves. Equal pay for equal work and the occasional pant-less hottie is all we ask. See also **double standard**.

etchings

Ironic excuse to invite some-one back to your place, as in "Would you like to come up and see my etchings?" It conveys a sense of humor and a sense of the absurd—because, duh, who has etchings?—both of which are undeniably sexy. It also does the hard work of introducing the idea of sex to the conversation without making things too heavy—and a light air always makes rejec-tion easier. Not to be confused with the clichéd and cheesy **"Would you like to come in for a nightcap?"**

ethical slut

❶ The title of a 1998 book subtitled *A Guide to Infinite Sexual Possibilities*, by Dossie Easton and Catherine A. Liszt—basically, *The Rules* for **polyamory** aficionados, but without the old-fashioned gen-der stereotypes, **game playing**, marriage panic, or divorced authors. Okay, so it's nothing like *The Rules*. ❷ A person who fucks honestly, ethically, and responsibly, without worrying about their **body count**. See also **slut**.

evangelism

Sex as a tool of change—e.g., a liberal screwing a Republi-can to swing their vote (à la Votergasm.com) or Tom Cruise falling in love to convert his girlfriends/wives to Scientology. However, it is more often seen as an after-the-fact plea, when one attempts to change one's partner's contrary (and there-fore despicable) opinions/

→

religion/philosophy/music tastes so one can justify continuing to boff them. A.k.a. sleeping with the enemy.

evidence

All the shit lying around your apartment that could significantly diminish your chances of getting laid, e.g. life-sized poster of Paula Abdul or Simon Cowell; prominently (and unironically) displayed college diploma or Little League trophy; a roommate à la Brad Pitt in *True Romance*; more than two bongs; more than two TVs; no TV; more than one teddy bear; economy-sized vat of lube (three-quarters empty); Billy Bass singing fish. See also **dry-run**.

eye candy

Something pleasing to the eye, intended to stimulate not the genitals but the *mind's* appreciation of beauty or sexiness. For example, an Abercrombie & Fitch or Victoria's Secret catalogue, gratuitous T&A shots in movies, trophy wives with plunging décolletage, Jude Law—all of these are mildly titillating but would never pass for pornography (unless, of course, you're 12 years old, in which case they're all primo masturbation material).

F

facial

Coming on someone's face, usually a woman's—though the act is popular in gay male porn, and *female* ejaculators can squirt on their partners during cunnilingus. Both are transmission fluids, so you should probably not be experimenting with facials with a new **casual sex** partner, even if **one-night stands** are the perfect venue for such acts of perversion (see **booty buzz**). And don't start whining to us about how nobody ever wears a condom or uses a dental dam during oral—*we know!* That doesn't mean *you* shouldn't. If everyone jumped off a bridge—oh, fuck it. Just be sure to get express permission before aiming your load at someone's kisser—that's just good manners.

fad sex

Position, sexual activity, or accessory that experiences a sudden increase in popularity due to a celebrity endorsement (see **Sting**), a magazine cover story (see **One Leg Up**), or a guest appearance on a major TV show (see the Rabbit on *Sex and the City*).

faking

❶ What every woman has done at least once in her lifetime. Pretending to climax is a theatrical art—one that even thespian/Method actor Keanu Reeves would find challenging to pull off convincingly. There's a healthy dose of heavy breathing with much melodramatic "oohing" and "ahhing" sprinkled throughout (all informed by porn and *When Harry Met Sally*) that builds to an Oscar-worthy crescendo, followed by a quick resolution phase ("That was great. Nightie-night!").

→

Faking is usually done for the benefit of a partner's ego, or simply to get said partner to roll over and go to sleep (*finally*). Though these are good intentions, no good can come of them. Faking begins a vicious cycle of deceit and miscommunication: Your partner thinks they gave you an orgasm with their patented moves, so they keep using those patented moves, thus you feel obliged to keep "responding" to them, until after a year of faking you finally break down and reveal your ruse out of pure exhaustion and boredom, at which point they break up with you because you've humiliated them with your damn lies! Why insist that sex be so goal oriented? It's not just sensualists and folk musicians who consider the journey to be as important as the destination. Climaxing is no more a prerequisite for great sex than wearing nice lingerie is. And, damn it, it's not easy for many women to get to their very own Xanadu. There's no simple formula like there is for most

dudes: insert, thrust, repeat. Female genitals are sensitive, fickle, and picky—and there's no shame in that. You've got to work with your partners, using honest communication, gentle instruction, and enthusiastic suggestion to teach them your parts' moods. That said, there is *one* instance when faking is acceptable: on a **one-night stand**, when you will not see this person again and, thus, there is no learning curve. In such a situation, giving yourself the freedom to *act* orgasmic may make you *feel* more orgasmic. (Hey, if forcing yourself to smile can make you feel happier . . .)

❷ What every man can do, too. Though it's a predominantly female phenomenon, don't think that men can't fake. Oh, yes they can—and do! A plethora of factors may contribute to a no-show: stress, depression, intoxication, relationship problems, medication, a thick condom—the list goes on. Add that to the overwhelming pressure of male ejaculatory expectation. Two or three

F

dramatic climactic thrusts, a quick removal of the condom in a darkened room, and his partner is none the wiser. Now you've got something new to obsess about the next time you're doing it with a dude.

faux no.

A fake telephone number given to someone hitting on you either because they are annoying and you want to humiliate them, because you're too much of a wuss to let them down gently, or because you just want them to go away. Popular sequences include your ex's number, Domino's, 867-5309, your own telephone number one digit off (e.g., you change the *7* to a *1* or the *0* to a *6* so you can claim they simply read it wrong should you meet again), or the **Rejection Hotline** number. See also **digits**.

Feminine Mystique, The

Book written by feminist Betty Friedan in 1963 that sparked a national debate about "the problem that has no name"—namely, the myth of the happy housewife/mother. It paved the way for all manner of "unfeminine" attitudes and behavior, including the embrace of birth control, premarital sex, dancing to the *Free to Be You and Me* album, the **zipless fuck**, and the **booty call**.

feng shui

❶ Arranging your bedroom furniture for optimum positive sexual energy. ❷ New Age bullshit disguised as an ancient Chinese secret that, if you publicly admit to subscribing to it, will significantly reduce your chances of getting laid.

flavor of the month

The person you're seeing–i.e., fucking–if you happen to go through partners like a box of tampons. They're called your "flavor of the moment" if you happen to go through partners like Kleenex.

fling

A bite-size relationship that's casual in retrospect but intense in the thick of it. A fling is usually monogamous, with lots of spooning and endorphin rushes that make you feel like you're in love, even though you know you're not. Flings typically have a built-in deadline– e.g., summer vacation, semester abroad, impending sex-change operation–and last no longer than a season. May come with one free sex toy. A.k.a. fun-size affair.

foreign accent

The perfect accessory for a **one-night stand**, an affair, or a **fling**. Preferably French– either real (Olivier Martinez in *Unfaithful*) or fake (*90210*'s Brenda during her semester abroad).

foreplay

The sexual equivalent of stretching before a big run–i.e., warming up. For women, this means 30 minutes of kissing, fondling, necking, teasing, whispering, nibbling, etc., before someone sticks something inside them. For men, this means 30 seconds of kissing before sticking their dick in something.

free love

What they used to call all this **hooking up** back in the sixties, when **casual sex** was just for hippies and communists.

F

free milk

A reference to the saying, "Why buy the cow when you can get the milk for free?" which translates to "Why get married (or make a **commitment**) to a woman when you can have sex with her first (i.e., without getting hitched)?" Charming.

frequency

The number of times you see a sex partner within any given period. This can make or break a **booty call** setup. More than once a week and you risk drifting into a **common-law relationship**. Less than once a year and the next time you call, their new spouse/parole officer/prayer partner might answer the phone.

friend with benefits

❶ *Adult usage:* A genuine pal whom you can occasionally call up for sex if neither of you is in a relationship. It's a kinder, gentler term than **fuck buddy**, and it usually applies to kinder, gentler people with these setups. ❷ *Teen usage:* What the kids these days call members of their incestuous inner circle. Traditional "boyfriends" or "girlfriends" with whom they might exclusively **go steady** have practically disappeared from the teen **dating** scene. A.k.a. booty buddy.

friend zone

A pigeonhole. Most of us sort new acquaintances into one of three categories: potential relationship, potential **hookup**, or friend zone. The major decision-making process of this categorization happens in the first few hours of meeting.

→

There are shuttle buses running fairly regularly between "potential relationship" and "potential hookup," but once you've been relegated to the friend zone, you may as well take your balls and go home. This area is heavily patrolled by such platitudes as "But I don't want to ruin our friendship" or, worse, "You're just so nice!" A.k.a. the **booty** black hole.

Friendster

❶ An online community (Friendster.com) that lets you feel like you've got more friends than you really do. It works in much the same way **STDs** spread: You sign up for an account, link to a friend's account, and are immediately linked up to that friend's group of friends. Pros: You can use it as an "in" to meet someone who moves in similar circles. Cons: Losers you've met *once* ask you to be their "friendster," putting you in the awkward position of either saying yes to a loser or saying no and looking like a total asshole. ❷ A second-tier acquaintance you shamelessly exploit for the access they provide you (to a supermodel, to the VIP room, to their famous mom, to their rooftop kiddie wading pool) even though you know they just like you for *you.*

fringe benefits

The nonwage portion of a relationship, or what they bring to the table in addition to making the Earth move for you—e.g., a **bartender** who comps your tab, a chef who feeds you, a trust fund brat who flies you to Paris on a whim, a hairdresser who comps your highlights, a sex writer who gets free sex-toy samples. (See *Em & Lo's Sex Toy: An A-to-Z Guide to Bedside Accessories* in a bookstore near you.) A.k.a. gravy.

F

frozen food aisle

The most common location referenced in a **Missed Connections** ad, probably because singles indulge in frozen TV dinners more often than couples do—e.g., "You were in the frozen food aisle of Key Food wearing a vintage Minnesota Wolverines T and a mischievous grin, I was fumbling with the Boca boxes. We bumped carts . . . accidentally? If not, let's go grocery shopping for a meal we can make together." See also **cereal aisle**.

fuck buddy

Someone with whom you have a relationship based solely on no-strings-attached sex. Unlike a **friend with benefits**, you would not call a fuck buddy just to talk if you got fired or your cat got run over, though you could probably hit them up for a loan if you were in a bind. However, the fact that the sex is usually naughtier—i.e., of the **doggy style** or **anal sex** variety—more than makes up for the lack of emotional connection. A.k.a. booty buddy.

fuck 'n' chuck

Postcoital breakup. Being on the receiving end of an f 'n' c ranks right up there with getting mugged, getting root canal surgery, and being dumped the day after you got mugged on your way home from the dentist's office.

fucksimile

❶ A person you sleep with simply because they remind you of (or are as close as you'll ever get to) someone you *really* want to fuck. ❷ Something like sex—e.g., cybersex, a RealDoll, or a large Ziploc baggie filled almost to capacity with lukewarm macaroni and cheese, one side of which is greased with butter, which you then wrap around your dick as you thrust, repeat.

F

G

game playing

Being two-faced in order to passive-aggressively manipulate a romantic or sexual scenario to your benefit. But we think if there's no board involved, you shouldn't be playing games. Here's an abridged how-to guide: Always be considerate and honest in your pursuit of **casual sex**. Mean what you say, and say what you mean. Avoid the practice of **unilateral casual sex**. Do not obsess about **hand**. Call when you say you'll call. Burn your copy of *The Rules*. Keep this encyclopedia on your coffee table.

gaydar

An innate ability to tell whether someone is gay. Especially useful during Freshman Week, at closing time if it's not a gay bar, in a relationship. Note: It's called gaydar only if you're gay or you like gay people. If you're homophobic, it's called "labeling any man who doesn't like NASCAR a faggot and any woman with short hair a feminazi." See also **playdar**.

George Michael, a

An anonymous public-bathroom dalliance.

girlfriend material

A woman who possesses the favorable qualities (a resemblance to Angelina Jolie, superb blow job acumen, child-bearing hips) that make her a good candidate for a long-term **commitment**, if he has anything to do with it, thus making him ask her to go steady as soon as possible (see **early decision**) so she'll immediately stop having sex with anyone other than him. See also **boyfriend material**.

glass ceiling

The arbitrary limit imposed on women (or that women impose on themselves, for that matter) to define sluthood. A man's **body count** can enter genocide territory and the worst he will be called is a **lady-killer**—or, in the modern vernacular, a **playa**. (Except by those ladies he has "slain," who will refer to him as Fuckface while continuing to find him irresistible.) A woman, on the other hand, barely has to hit double digits before being called easy, sleazy, or a ho-bag. See also **double standard**, **reputation**, **slut**.

glory hole

The fist-size hole between booths in the back of adult book/video stores or between stalls in public restrooms (usually at truck stops) through which penises can be stuck for anonymous hand jobs, blow jobs, or **anal sex**. Apparently, there's a whole protocol of nonverbal negotiations and actions for such dalliances, not least of which is the silent insistence on condom use. The initiated swear that horror stories (outside of the spread of **STDs**) are mere urban legends, but we'd still recommend jabbing your dick in your own ear before sticking it in a glory hole.

going out

Like **going steady**, but with the monogamous exchange of bodily fluids instead of class rings.

going steady

❶ Monogamous **dating**, typically signaled by the exchange of class rings, that doesn't necessarily involve the exchange of bodily fluids. This arcane term, left over from the age of beehives and misogyny, is best applied today to True Love Waits members, who exchange silver keys, instead of class rings, as a promise (and helpful reminder) that their virginity is under lock and key (that is, until 6 months from now, when she gets drunk and does it without a condom because she never learned how to effectively protect herself against pregnancy and ends up having to get an abortion paid for by Mummy, who happens to head up the local pro-life committee, because no daughter of hers is going to have some bastard out of wedlock). ❷ Ironic hipster term for a couple dating exclusively.

gold digging/ gold digger

❶ A get-rich-quick scheme that has nothing to do with Cutco knives. Whether the agreement is unspoken (as with gold digging **flings** or relationships) or outlined in legal documents (as with gold digging marriages), one party, known as the **arm candy**, agrees to perform various services (sexual and perhaps culinary) in exchange for diamonds, a house in the Hamptons, haute couture, and BMWs. Patron saints: Anna Nicole Smith and John Kerry. Poor man's substitute: Darva Conger. This type saw its latest 15 minutes via reality TV, in particular *Joe Millionaire, Who Wants to Marry a Millionaire*, and Jerry Hall's *Kept*. Teenage gold digger wannabes with a high-speed **Internet** connection

→

are known as cam girls—pretty young things who giggle in front of their webcams or publish photos of themselves scantily clad in exchange for gifts off their Amazon wish list. Like many things teen and "cool," the cam-girl phenomenon has its roots in Japan, where tens of thousands of school girls practice *enjo kosai*, or "compensated dating"; these girls next door are willing to dine out with older men, and maybe even grant sexual favors, to support their shopping habit. Go, girl power, go! ❷ Alternative, not-safe-for-TV definition: A gold digger is someone who doesn't ask whether you've showered recently before ringing your back-door bell with a pinkie or more (sorry, Mom).

Google

❶ The magical way you "happen" to know your ex just married a ballerina, recently developed an allergy to nuts, and/or is starting to lose his hair. ❷ A good reason *not* to post online any of the following: naked self-portraits, your true feelings about your in-laws, poetry.

Google, to

To engage in amateur detective work on the **Internet** to sniff out a new paramour's published works, criminal record, charity affiliations, naked self-portraits, or past association with a medieval-reenactment society.

Google-gänger

A play on *doppelgänger*: Someone who shares your name and is frequently mistaken for you

G

by new acquaintances with a **Google** habit. Particularly embarrassing if your Google-gänger has questionable political leanings, an unusually strong interest in wizards and elves, or a fledgling career as an amateur porn star.

Google goggles

The rose-tinted glasses through which one views a new paramour after an exhaustive **Internet** search on them yields very impressive results: a book written in the Amazon top 100, a library wing named after them, a gorgeous portrait taken by Herb Ritz, a Pulitzer, etc. But though they may be good on paper (or, should we say, on Web pages), they may not be good for you in person. Your Google goggles may prevent you from recognizing this before you agree to a second date or to sex, whichever comes first. See also **beer goggles**.

gossip

A Darwinian mechanism that curbs unethical sluttiness. Frequently abused to punish entirely **ethical slut**-tiness, especially when this behavior is witnessed in Southern Baptists or women. A.k.a. the grapevine, the rumor mill, trial by watercooler.

grief therapy

Any kind of sensual or sexual embrace that gives one comfort, connects one with the cycle of life, makes one feel alive, takes one's mind off an all-consuming grief, or simply jolts one out of a sense of numbness after the devastating loss of a friend, family member, or lover. The person in mourning should feel no shame about yearning for mourning sex—it's a natural urge. Those not in mourning offering up said comfort should not take advantage of the mourner's delicate state, nor should they expect this to be the beginning ➔

of a beautiful relationship:
You're a selfless surrogate, a
mercy fucker, a sexual social
worker, a pint of ice cream,
and nothing more. A.k.a. post-
traumatic sex. See also **comfort sex**.

Groucho Marx syndrome

Not wanting to belong to a club
that would accept you as a
member—i.e., finding it a turn-
off when someone likes you too
much, or wanting only those
you can't have.

G

group sex

When more than three people
do the nasty together. The term
"group sex" usually implies a
convivial and jaunty attitude
among all participants and a
spontaneous beginning—i.e.,
the kind of **orgy** that might
result from a particularly saucy
game of Twister. See also **play
party, One Leg Up, three-way**.

H

Halloween

The perfect opportunity to **dress up**, act, and fuck like someone you're not: a French maid, a superhero, a crack whore, Michael Jackson—wait, scratch that last one.

hand

Short for the term "upper hand," usually used in the context of relationships. The word was made famous by the *Seinfeld* episode in which George Costanza, under the illusion that he is in the romantic power position, can't believe *he's* being dumped and exclaims "But I've got hand!" to which his now ex-girlfriend replies, "And you're gonna need it." Gaining hand is particularly important for some people (the insecure **game playing** types of the world) in the early stages of **hooking up** or **dating** who, in attempt to gain it, might flirt outrageously with the **bartender** during a **Schrödinger's date**, purposely postpone returning a call, or be suddenly "unavailable" on a Saturday night. But here's the rub: If you, like Costanza, feel the need to actively pursue hand or boast that you have it, you don't have it. Those who actually *do* have hand probably never even heard of the concept.

handbag

❶ A purse that doubles as an overnight kit for a single woman on the make: Her Fendi baguette will easily hold **condoms**, **lube**, toothbrush, spare undies, lipstick, **business card**s, gum, cell phone, and, if she was once a Girl Scout, a cock ring ("Be prepared!").
❷ What women **dance** around when they're out on a **ladies' night**, because there are no men to keep an eye on all the Kate Spades, and because groups of

→

women *always* dance in a circle (see also **bachelorette party**). ❸ Litmus test for a straight man's sexual security factor: When his date asks him to hold her pastel pink pocketbook while she either pees, dances to "It's Raining Men" with the girls, or holds back her friend's hair while she pukes, does he adamantly refuse, does he hold it at arm's length like it's a soiled diaper, or does he slip it over his shoulder with an affable grin? There is a direct correlation between his comfort level with holding a handbag and how supportive he is of marriage rights for gays, how his mama raised him, and how amenable he'll be to a little backdoor "reach-around" with a pinkie (or more). ❹ A way for a woman to mark her territory, if you ask a **ladies' man**: He may get relationship panic if she asks him to hold her bag while she pees, convinced that she's doing it only to ward off any competitors in her absence.

handcuffs

Police-issue (or costume store-bought) restraining device worn around the wrists. Like any other piece of **bondage** equipment, handcuffs are a really, really, *really* bad idea on a **one-night stand** with someone you just met, during breakup sex (if you were the dumper), or with someone whose heart you broke at any time in the past. Besides, metal handcuffs can cause serious injury—better to go with purpose-made Velcro cuffs, which are more comfy and easier to get out of.

hanging out

A one-size-fits-all description of a sexual or **dating** scenario that's purposely vague in order to absolve one of romantic responsibilities or expectations, as in "Oh, you know Caitlin?" "Yeah, we've been hanging out." See also **dating, going out, going steady, hooking up.**

happy ending

A massage session at a massage parlor (usually in Chinatown) wherein the masseur or masseuse rubs your genitals just as unceremoniously as he or she rubs your shoulders. Once the genital rubbing begins (sans eye contact, **dirty talk**, or subtlety), their fancy fingerwork usually elicits an orgasm within 5–7 seconds. A.k.a. happy finish.

hate fucking

When lust trumps like. Sex with someone who annoys you is a drag, but sex with someone you hate with every pore of your being? Now, that's hot. Not on a regular basis, of course (that's just depressing), but sometimes it's just what the shrink ordered. Push each other around, pull each other's hair, bite each other's shoulders, and yell, "I fucking hate you!" right as you come. It's like an enema for the soul. Now go sit in a warm bath with a pint of Ben & Jerry's Rocky Mountain Road or a glass of Scotch and call your mama.

H

he's just not that into you

❶ The title of a best-selling self-help book for women with self-destructive **dating** habits whose entire thesis is encapsulated in the title and milked for the next 176 pages. **❷** The reason he's not calling you, not introducing you to his friends, not having sex with you—read the aforementioned book if you need it spelled out for you.

heartbreak sex

The sexual equivalent of a Vicodin. When it hurts so bad that you wonder how you ever found knock-knock jokes funny, and you're too afraid of your addictive personality to self-medicate, but you wish to God you could think about something other than the adorable creature who just ran over your heart with a Humvee, sometimes the only thing to do is seek out an orgasm. As long as there's a **prenook** involved,

we see nothing wrong with this, though we don't recommend indulging in it more than once per breakup. See also **comfort sex**, **grief therapy**, **I-deserve-it sex**, **metabolize**, **rebound**.

herpes

A popular—no, that's the wrong word—a *common* virus that infects one in five Americans, one-third of whom don't even know they have it, since many carriers never get symptoms. Those who *do* get symptoms are the unhappy hosts to recurring, contagious, painful, oozing sores that last about a week (or three) on either the genitals or the mouth. There's no cure and no vaccine, though it can be *managed* with prescription meds and healthy living, allowing you to resume your vigorous sex life. Still, you should know that something called "asymptomatic shedding" (i.e., spreading without the presence of symptoms), though rare, does occur—but there's no way to know when. And since it

H

→

can affect the skin around the genitals, condoms will reduce the risk but won't obliterate it. Bummer. Call the National Herpes Hotline (919-361-8488) or visit ashastd.org/hrc for more deets.

hickey

A bruise caused by someone living out their Dracula fantasy on your bod. The hickey is, at its heart, a territory marker, and therefore one would think it would be unwelcome during **casual sex**, which is all about self-ruling countries. But one would be wrong. Certainly, the neck hickey should be adminis-

tered only with *explicit* permission, and it would be wrong to take advantage of someone's diminished capacities—i.e., drunken stupor—to extract an "Oh, God, yes, please vacuum my neck." But don't be surprised if your **one-night stand** actually requests a *passion purpura*—the kids these days seem to wear them with ironic pride, much as they might an old Wham! concert tee. If you're enjoying sex for sex's sake and you're not an investment banker or a bereavement counselor, why *not* brag, nonverbally, about the crazy sex you're having? If that's a little ostentatious for your liking, try a hickey below the neck for a saucy all-day note to self that you got some last night. You may find such a reminder too sad after **heartbreak sex** and too unsettling after **hate fucking**, but after a good bout of **I-deserve-it sex** or **I've-still-got-it sex**, it's a giggle. On a final note, if you discover during a make-out **sesh** that the person you're sucking face with is married or in a so-called monogamous setup (perhaps their wedding band falls out of their pocket, or they say, "I can't stay the night, because the old ball-and-chain gets suspicious"), feel free to give them a neck hickey the size of Ohio before kicking them to the curb.

himbo

The male equivalent of a bimbo. See also **slut**, **double standard**.

hit that

As in "I'd hit that." A cocky way of announcing, usually to a friend, that you're into someone sexually, implying that you would give them the privilege of fucking you, if only you had the time. Literally meaning "penetrate those female genitals with my tiny dick," the term is used almost exclusively by male heterosexuals wearing some form of head gear. While they may think this phrase makes them sound like macho studs, more evolved bystanders will assume the speakers spend most nights in their depressing little apartments poking a plastic replica of Jenna Jameson's pussy that they bought online from Xandria.com for $29.99. Its sister term is "tap that," as in "I'd like to tap that ass," most likely coined by frat guys of yore who drank away their ability to distinguish between a keg and a woman.

HIV

The sexually transmitted virus that causes AIDS. Not to be flippant, but the biggest problem with HIV is that people assume it's *so* early nineties. As drug therapy has improved and people are living with HIV rather than dying from it, HIV has come to be considered a lifelong but manageable disease, in the vein of, say, diabetes. And, as the AIDS stories recede from the front pages, so people have become more lax about **safe(r) sex**. We bet you'll never guess how this story ends: At the beginning of the twenty-first century, the number of new HIV diagnoses among gay men started to increase for the first time in years. The rate has remained relatively stable in the rest of the population—but "stable" is still a long way from "low," especially among minority women and needle sharers. The recent rise in HIV among gay men has been attributed partly to the crystal meth epidemic (apparently, four-day drug 'n' club binges lead to unsafe **casual sex**—who knew?), and partly to the feeling that things can only get better. Let's get the party restarted! Well, here's a front-page story for ya: A million Americans are infected with HIV, and there's still no cure. Put *that* in your meth pipe and smoke it. See also **[blank] dick, booty bump, safe(r) sex, STDs, STD ennui**.

home game

Couch potato sex. There you are, having a quiet night in: Domino's pizza, chamomile tea, and the complete first season of *The Office* on DVD (the original BBC version, of course). You brush your teeth, floss (twice), put on your flannel PJs, and settle in for a good 9 hours' sleep, when you suddenly get *that* itch, combined with the indubitable feeling that polishing your own china just won't cut it. If, at this point, from your bed, you place a **booty call** and actually manage to convince someone to leave the **bar** or get out of their own bed to join you, then, my friend, you are playing a home game. And may we add what a serious **player** you are, too? Plus: look, ma, no hangover! A.k.a. ordering in.

home-team advantage

When your own turf, whether that's your bedroom or your local **bar**, helps you get laid and/or make a lasting impression. Perhaps she thinks you're just a **himbo** and then wakes up to see Dostoyevsky on your

→

H

→ nightstand, for example. (Make sure you've at least read the Cliff's Notes first.) Or maybe he thinks you're a timid book-worm, and then the **bartender** happens to mention that you're a shark on the pool table. During a **one-night stand**, the home-team advantage means you don't have to lie there won-dering whether your presence is welcome until sunup (though this may turn into a home-team *dis*advantage if you find your-self in a **coyote ugly** situation, longing to sneak out).

casual nature of a relationship may use the term "hooking up," even though intercourse *was* had. Hooking up systematically replaced the **date** as the main form of romantic interaction among single people during the last quarter of the twentieth century, hence the slight confu-sion over the term: For those born before 1965, it means just meeting up or getting together, nonsexually; Gen-Xers prefer *our* definition (natch); and those under 30 use it to denote anything from a French kiss to rimming. A.k.a. fooling around.

hooking up

A vague and amorphous set of romantic and sexual interactions that defies definition, rule setting, expectations, and old-fashioned gender stereotypes. But if we *had* to define it, we'd say it meant casual sexual relations between two people, ranging anywhere from a make-out **sesh** to **oral sex** but *not* including penetration with a penis or dildo. However, those wishing to emphasize the

hosting

Adult sleepovers—or, why there should be a *Martha Stewart Fucking* magazine. We don't care if you're hung like a porn star, if you give blow jobs that guys rave about for weeks, or if you're more giving in bed than a career masochist—you've still got to be a good host when you're entertaining for one. And this doesn't just apply to those who could possibly be

→

the One—this applies to **one-night stands**, **booty calls**, spontaneous **three-ways**, the lot. The consummate shag palace should be furnished with a spare toothbrush (still in its package), **condoms** and/or dental dams, a guest pillow, and **lube**. In addition, some ladies who are particularly self-conscious about hairy pits/legs may find themselves at your place, having not expected to get lucky that night. Said ladies may go scrambling in your bathroom for a razor and end up scraping their legs with a rusty, weeks-old Schick. Do them a favor and leave a good razor and shaving foam in plain view. Not that *you* should care, of course—you're about to get lucky, so will stubbly legs *really* ruin the moment?—but some girls are funny like that. If you really want to make a lasting impression, postcoital snacks and/or breakfast are a nice touch, too (for the record, Ice Pops are the former, not the latter). In addition, the host should pay attention to details such as clean sheets, clean bath-room, cool tunes, and mood lighting. And there should be no obvious signs of other current or past partners—e.g., Y-fronts on the kitchen floor, cutesy **Post-it notes** on the night-stand, framed photos of exes on the wall—even if it is just a one-night stand with a **prenook** or an open **booty call** situation. That's just rude. If you have a home phone and are in the habit of receiving late-night booty calls, turn down the volume on your answering machine. It has come to our attention that some male pony-tailed **players** (an odd and, some would say, beguiling combination) keep tampons on hand, too, in case their guests receive an unexpected visit from Aunt Flow. Some girls might find this charming in a New Age-y, **free love** kind of way, but we just think it's weird. On a final note, if you invite someone over to your place for dinner, don't *ever* cut the pota-toes and carrots into little heart shapes (oh, it happens). See also **feng shui**.

H

HPV

It's #1! The most common sexually transmitted virus, that is. More than 75 percent of Americans will have an HPV (human papillomavirus) infection at some point, whether they know it or not. And it's hard to know, since many people are never symptomatic (though they may be contagious), it's not that easy to test for in guys, and the virus may come and go, depending on an individual's immune system. There are many, many different strains of HPV—some cause low-risk visible warts on the external genital areas, while others result in microscopic abnormal internal or external cell changes that can sometimes lead to cancer (mostly in women). Though there's no cure, the affected skin and cells can be removed and intimidated, via healthy living, from coming back. Whatever kind of sex you have, whether it's casual or not, you're likely to run into HPV if you or your partner has had more than one previous partner. For more info, visit ashastd.org. See also **safe(r) sex, STDs**.

humor

If you don't find **casual sex** funny, you're missing the point. Seriously, lighten the fuck up. If you need a reminder of exactly how funny it is, watch your orgasm face in the mirror next time you're doing the dirty.

hypnosis

An artificially induced trance, characterized by heightened suggestibility and receptivity to direction. A professional hypnotist may be hired to help someone feel subconsciously sexier (perhaps by convincing them that their boobs have been hypnotized up two cup sizes). A pathetic loser might buy a kit off the Web to learn how to unwittingly hypnotize chicks into sleeping with him. Instead of scoring, though, he simply ends up feeling, subconsciously, like even more of a loser. See also **pickup artists**.

H

I-can't-believe-it's-not-boinking

Anything that feels just as good as intercourse, **oral sex**, or **anal sex**—but isn't. This could include an hour-long massage (with or without a **happy ending**), an amazing death-by-chocolate dessert, a two-hour make-out **sesh** the likes of which you haven't experienced since junior high, or a drunken night of **dry humping** and fondling. Though it's primarily—almost exclusively—a "female thing," the occasional man in love has been known to get his jollies this way, basking in the novelty of delayed gratification, assuming he is the first man ever to feel this way, and marveling to himself, "I can't believe how much fun all that making out was—it wasn't even boinking!" Straight girls, on the other hand, can enjoy I-can't-believe-it's-not-boinking on a merely casual basis. Wary of the **glass ceiling**, rampant **STDs**, and the unlikelihood that 5 minutes of jackhammering is going to do it for her, a girl may take a boy home from a **bar**, engage in some heavy petting (with or without release), serve him some Eggos, and show him the door—not because she's playing games or holding out for girl-friend status, but because that's all she needs, thank you very much. See also **blue balls**.

I-deserve-it sex

Sex intended to boost your self-confidence or self-esteem, usually after a long, dry spell or a particularly bad day, with some-one you would normally feel bad about shagging (because they're married or ugly).

"I'll call you"

The most frequently abused phrase in the entire dating patois. Let's break this down, shall we? If you say, "I'll call you," freakin' call already. If bonobos would fly out of your arse before you dialed that particular number, be a man (or woman) about it, and say something generic and noncommittal like "I had a lovely time" or "See you around" or "Thanks for the rim job!" If you panic and blurt out these three little words in order to speed your getaway, you should at least drop that person an email or **text message** to say, "I had a lovely time. See you around, and thanks for the rim job." Yeah, right: *That'd* be nice. But let's be honest: Pat Robertson will appear on *The Ellen Degeneres Show* before careless hooker-uppers stop lying through their teeth about whether they'll call. So, if someone says, "I'll call you," and doesn't, they probably didn't lose your number, experience a sudden death in the family, get unfairly jailed for protesting the destruction of the rain forest, or get trapped under a heavy object. Sure, you can go ahead and call them once to rule out all of the above—because once a decade, someone does lose the number of someone they dig—but after that, move on, friend. Don't call me once, shame on you; don't call me twice, shame on me. See also **he's just not that into you**.

I've-still-got-it sex

Sex intended to prove to the world (read: yourself) that you're still sexy, good looking, in shape, youthful, and/or adventurous, even though you're bland, ugly, fat, old, and/or boring.

IM

Instant messaging—i.e., a way for someone to be notified the *second* you log on to your computer so they can send you an IM mere *seconds* afterward:

→

"Hey, you free tonight?" Need we explain why you should give out your IM handle to your closest friends and long-term partners *only*? Sure, you might be ready to show each other your **assholes**, but are you sure you're ready for an IM **commitment**? We recommend waiting until after the "Let's **go steady**" conversation before adding each other to your IM Buddy List.

Internet

A revolutionary technological advancement whose main purpose is to give people the ability to easily and anonymously troll for sex, including but not limited to online pornography, erotica, cybersex chat rooms, and adult personal sites. Its virtual network connects anyone with a computer and a dial-up/DSL to anyone else with the same, so that freaks like 41-year-old Armin Meiwes of Germany can find someone like 43-year-old Bernd-Jurgen

Brandes to let him cut off his penis, flambé it, eat it (*together*), and then kill him. God bless technology! A.k.a. the information superhighway, the World Wide Web. See also **online personals**.

Internets

Same term as above, but mistakenly used by old people who don't quite grasp the concept, or ironically used by irreverent dot-com kids to compensate for their earnestness when discussing geek matters.

intimacy lite

If you've ever spooned your booty call or held hands with your **one-night stand**, you're familiar with intimacy lite. If both parties are fully onboard with the "lite" nature of the intimacy, it's perfectly natural—everyone needs a **cuddle** sometimes, and even the most ardent **commitment-phobe**

→

among us misses snuggling and nuzzling and—eww, okay, we'll stop. Commitment-phobes are *especially* prone to indulging in intimacy lite, and this often sends a mixed message, because if your mouth is saying one thing and your body is saying another, your partner is going to listen to whichever message they like best. Sure, you might have agreed in the **prenook** that the sex wouldn't mean anything, but does **brunch** invalidate a prenook? Not in our book (that'd be this one), but plenty of tender-hearted young things out there might think so. All crushed up, they refuse to believe that sometimes, someone simply needs help finishing the crossword, or wants company at brunch because all their good friends are brunching with their significant others or shopping at Pottery Barn. To make a sweeping generalization (Who, *us*? Never!), men are most often the culprits in cases of mis-understood intimacy lite, perhaps because they dominate

the ranks of the commitment-phobic. It's not just getting **free milk**—it's having Bessie listen to you ramble on about your problems at work, too: a mini-me relationship on tap, whenever you need a top-up. But, hey, if you can cross your hearts and swear on your mothers' graves that you two **fuck buddies** *both* enjoy a little postcoital grocery shop-ping, don't let us keep you from the **frozen food aisle**. A.k.a. casual intimacy. Someone who regularly engages in intimacy lite is known as a **sampler**.

J

jealousy

The green-eyed monster. Though, as far as monsters go, it's more on the Snuffleupagus end of the spectrum. After all, as long as it doesn't reach stalker or Taliban proportions, a little jealousy can be cute. It shows you care. You'll hear the poo-pooers whine about jealousy being uncivilized, a reflection of insecurity or possessiveness. But jealousy is like masturbation: Ninety percent of people say they experience it, and the other 10 percent are lying. Either that, or they've never been in love. Sad, really.

judging

Thinking poorly of people who don't act like you, think like you, or fuck like you.

juggling

The delicate act of managing multiple relationships/sex partners without lying, sending mixed messages, or accidentally shouting out the wrong name during sex. See also **open relationship**, **polyamory**.

jumping the shark

This phrase refers to the moment you *should* have called the relationship quits, though it ended up taking you another few hours/days/weeks/months/years to follow through. The term, coined by a bunch of college friends, refers to the *Happy Days* episode in which Fonzie literally jumped over a shark on water skis, and is usually applied to the moment a pop-culture phenom takes a one-way trip down the crapper, like when Mariah Carey starred in *Glitter*. (Of course, the phrase itself jumped the shark a good

→

4 years ago, when a book of the same name was published.) As far as relationships go, you know your blind date has jumped the shark when one of you asks, "So, what color is *your* parachute?" Your **one-night stand** has jumped the shark when one of you whines about the condom/can't get it up/pukes/points and laughs when the undies come off/won't return the favor/suggests water sports. Your **booty call** has jumped the shark when you meet up and just watch *The Daily Show* together instead of shagging like rabbits. Your relationship has jumped the shark when the way they chew makes you want to punch them in the face.

just friends

A defensive description of a supposedly platonic relationship. If you're "just friends," you never really *are* "just friends," are you? Because if you were, you'd be "friends." Period. "Just friends" implies that your friendship is under external review and you are therefore forced to insist (to your friend/"friend"/partner/parent) that you and s/he are "just friends." But come on now, you can tell us—are you *sure* you're *just* friends? Before you get all prickly on us, "just friends" doesn't necessarily mean you're making whoopee together—it simply implies that the friendship is a little, shall we say, complicated. Either a) you used to make whoopee, b) one of you would kinda maybe like to make whoopee, c) you both kind of know you'll eventually make whoopee, or d) you spend so much time together that you may as well be making whoopee—what the hell's stopping you, anyway? Didn't you see *When Harry Met Sally*?

J

K

karma

The Eastern philosophical belief that if you cheat on me and consequently give me genital **herpes**, you *will* be in a horrible accident involving the removal of your body from your penis.

key party

❶ If you believe Rick Moody's novel *The Ice Storm* or its film adaptation, this was a rather gloomy preamble to sleeping with your neighbor's spouse back in the suburbs of the seventies. Moody's key parties were fraught with scheming, lying, cheating, alcoholism, buffet snacking, and sudden, tragic death. ❷ Something your parents definitely *never* participated in. Honestly. Would we lie to you? ❸ A suburban legend.

kiss

The most perfect, compact, indicative, and predictive sex act there is. We're willing to bet that if you like each other's kiss, you'll like the hard-core butt pirating even more. And in a relationship that's close to **jumping the shark**, kissing is the first thing to go. Yes, we learned all this from *Pretty Woman*.

kiss & tell

Blabbing about your exploits. When a girl does it, it's a bonding experience, a sharing of

→

emotion, a mutual exchange of tips and techniques, and an exploration of the human sexual condition. When a guy does it, it's an attempt to make soda come out his friend's nose by recounting how he fucked the shit out of this girl, literally: "A little nugget of poo actually came out!"

kissing bandit

❶ She's a Southern gal with a hyphenated name like Nancy-Claire or Ann-Margaret. She was a little tubby in high school—not so fat that the other kids threw stuff at her, but just curvy enough to be excluded from all the **dating** rituals. Her deb ball was an exercise in public humiliation, and her pink ruffled dress was three sizes larger than any of the other gowns on display. After graduation, she was accepted to a good ol' Southern school like Emory, lost twenty pounds during freshman year when her roommate showed her how to "pull her trigger," and suddenly realized that she's quite cute, actually. She learned to measure her cuteness in male attention and flirted with abandon, and then, after one too many So-Co-and-Diet-Cokes, she realized making out is easy, fun, and calorie free. By junior year, she was fully dependent on sucking face at least once a night out to remind herself how cute she got. She'll never go all the way, of course, because she'd really like to save herself for someone special (okay, so she'd like the *second* guy she sleeps with to be someone special—how could she have known that Chad from Alabama would turn out to be such a jerkface sophomore year?). ❷ A gal who's hooked on **I-can't-believe-it's-not-boinking**. ❸ Anyone on ecstasy. See also **CAKE parties**, **herpes**.

L

ladies' man

❶ Ladies' men like the ladies, *aw yeah*. Al Green would be a ladies' man if he weren't a reverend. (Actually, Al is more like the ultimate **wingman**, come to think of it—a singing Cyrano, if you will.) Ladies' men are possessed of a George Clooney-esque charm, though they may not necessarily be blessed with George Clooney-esque looks. In fact, the only trait all ladies' men share is an unshakeable confidence in their own sex appeal. They flirt shamelessly—not always with intent, but often simply because they enjoy leaving a trail of giggly, blushing women in their wake. Ladies' men can make a 90-year-old widow feel like a schoolgirl. They compliment, compliment, compliment, and it (almost) always feels sincere. They seem genuinely interested in women—what makes ladies laugh, what

cheers them up, what makes them weak at the knees, what makes them feel desired. They often declare publicly and earnestly, "I love women" (a serious shortcoming). And they *do* love women, *plural*. Afflicted with romantic ADD, they lack focus; if monogamous, they are serially so (we're talking triple digits). Still, ladies' men tend to be nicer than **players**, **cads**, or **roger dodgers**, who would never flirt simply for the sake of flirting. **Players** and their ilk flirt to fuck and often succeed less by being charmers than by being **assholes** (which, as we all know, lame women find irresistible). But ladies' men, on the other hand, might actually prefer a trip to Barney's with the girls than an afternoon at a sports **bar** with the boys. Because while players and cads and roger dodgers may chase waifish model types around the bar (see **modelizers**), ladies' men like what girls are really made of—not sugar and spice, but boobs, hips, asses, curves, and emotions. They make fabulous best pals—especially if

→

there aren't enough gay men in your town for every girl to have her own GBF (gay best friend)— though they make frustrating, thoughtless, very *un*charming boyfriends. Ladies' men that we can't help but like, just a little, include Bill Clinton, Colin Farrell, **Alfie**, Tom Jones, Thomas from Kundera's *The Unbearable Lightness of Being*. ❷ If he's too old to be a player— or if you're too old to refer to someone as a player—he's a ladies' man.

ladies' night

❶ A women-only* group outing of friends intended to promote heart mending, bonding, and/ or girl power. Ladies' night is an excuse to express your inner turmoil or joy through the medium of dance (a uniquely feminine need). It's an excuse to get smashed on Cosmos and end up teary eyed and nause-ated while you confess your deepest fears or sins (like how you fucked your best friend's

boyfriend 5 years ago, while they were still together). It's an excuse to get dressed up and make men eat their hearts out (though, depending on the number of Cosmos consumed, one member of a ladies' night will probably end up with a man eating *her* out if the group allows him to infiltrate its ranks). See also **bachelorette party, handbag.** ❷ A popular **bar** promotion allowing women to drink free in order to attract more male paying customers who assume the female clientele will end up wasted enough to be date rape-able.

Female impersonators count.

lady-killer

An old-fashioned term for **player** or **playa**.

last call

A **bartender**'s announcement signaling that, ladies and gentlemen, the time for gathering **digits** is over—it's **booty calling** time! **Designated dialers**, take your positions. **One-night-standers**, have you signed your **prenooks**? Everybody, please tip your **bartenders** generously. None of this would be possible without them. So, uh, where's the after-party? A.k.a. the witching hour (since you're more likely to go home with a hag at this time of night). See also **coyote ugly**.

last wo/man on Earth

The person you wouldn't sleep with even if he or she was the yadda yadda yadda . . . . Every good citizen should be familiar with their close friends' particular last man and last woman on Earth (i.e., minors, Republicans, drug addicts, people who still live with their parents). These people are, inexplicably (or perhaps very explicably), frequently the ones lingering longest after **last call**. In severe cases of **beer goggles**, combined with a particularly harsh **bear market**, your friends may be tempted to leave the **bar** with their "last wo/man on Earth." *You must stop them.* Feel free to employ arm locks, fake asthma attacks, and outbursts (within earshot of said last wo/man) about your friend's scorching case of crabs.

layaway

❶ Investments of time, effort, money, hair waxing, etc., that you make in order to convince a certain someone to sleep with you. For example, if you're a hairy hippie with an eye on a yuppie WASP, your layaway plan might include shaving, adding some Ralph Lauren to your wardrobe, and drinking gin and tonics at noon in order to make yourself

→

more attractive to the object of your affection. ❷ Saving up money to eventually hire a high-end escort. ❸ Fucking out of town. A.k.a. **out-of-towner**.

Alex ★★★★ 555-9901
nympho

Sandy ★★★ 555-3871
cute but needy

CC ★ 555-6678
bunny boiler

Randy (aka SUSH) ★★★
555-8992 so ugly she's hot

little black book *(archaic)*

❶ Back in the days before cell phones, **speed dial**, Blackberries, **email**, **IM**, and personal assistants, **ladies' men**, **players**, **playas**, **kissing bandits**, and daters in general needed somewhere to keep all their **digits**. Hence, the little black book. The main advantage of a little black book was that it didn't

engender **drunk dialing**. By the time you got to a phone, you were generally more in the mood for a slice of pizza, a glass of warm milk, and your own bed. ❷ Now that we are living in a digital world, "little black book" is more frequently employed as a metaphorical allusion to the number of **luvvas** one has in **rotation**. As in, "So, who's in your little black book these days?" ❸ Your **body count**. ❹ A movie starring Brittany Murphy that we *pray to God* we never get stuck watching on a transatlantic flight.

loopholing

When a person engages either in **casual sex** with a previous partner (see **returning to the well**) or in **outercourse** with a new partner for the *sole* purpose of keeping their **body count** static (as opposed to doing the above out of habit, or for the sheer pleasure, or because of easy access, etc.). A.k.a. retarded. See also **anal sex**.

LTR

Long-term relationship. (Come on, that was a gimme.)

lube

A teaspoon of "sugar" that helps the condom go down (if you put a drop on the inside) as well as in and out (if you put a few drops on the outside).

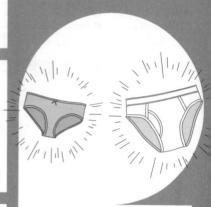

lucky underwear

Your grandmother was right: You should *always* wear nice undies. Because your odds of getting some tonight are way higher than your odds of getting hit by a bus and ending up in an ambulance in your skivvies (though your mom did always want you to marry a doctor). Your lucky underwear is a subset of "nice undies"— it's that pair that hugs your package or your butt cheeks just so, the pair that helps you radiate charm and sex appeal, the pair you always seem to be wearing when you get lucky, the pair you dance around your living room in when "You Sexy Thing," by Hot Chocolate, comes on the radio. Always wear your lucky undies on a first or blind date—even if, or perhaps especially if, you don't want things to get too hot and heavy just yet. Your lucky underwear is not just a scoring device—it's your pocketful of kryptonite, baby, and it makes you sparkle. But do us all a

→

favor, would you? Save something for later: It spoils the fun if we can see three inches of your lucky thong above your super-lo-rise jeans (*so* 5 minutes ago), or if we can tell you're wearing tighty-whities because you forgot to zip your fly after you peed. See also **plot spoiler.**

LUG (lesbian until graduation)

The sexual orientation of approximately one-half of college girls. In high school, they identify as straight, **dating** the captain of the football team and dutifully submitting to his clumsy and fairly unsatisfying fondling in the back seat of his dad's Range Rover. Once in college, they take a women's studies class on French feminist lesbian lit and subsequently begin to wonder about the same sex—namely, how a woman's lips and boobies might feel. Drunk with their newfound freedom and just plain drunk, they finally kiss a girl (with tongue) in order to a) satisfy their curiosity, b) privately rebel against their Republican "family values" parents, and/or c) challenge society's restrictive "norms" and thus create a more harmonious and beautiful world. It's a phase they outgrow when they put on the cap and gown. See also **BUT (bi-curious until thirty), kissing bandit.**

luvva

The only spelling of *lover* we can stomach.

M

marking (your) territory

❶ Ejaculating on someone's face or bed sheets. ❷ Giving your partner a **hickey** that can't be easily covered by clothing. ❸ Leaving clothes (especially undergarments), personal photos of yourself, your toiletries, or any other personal item at a sex partner's home in order to make the following statement to said partner or any visitor they may have over: "I'm an important sexual fixture here; don't underestimate the wrath I can wield if scorned. I'll be back tomorrow. Miss me!" ❹ Giving someone your school pin or varsity jacket, presenting an engagement ring, exchanging wedding bands, clothes shopping for a partner at stores that reflect your style (not theirs), getting matching tattoos.

masturbation

It means never having to say you're sorry. And it means never having to wait by the phone, say **"I'll call you"** and not mean it, do the **walk of shame**, ask, "What was your name again?" sign a **prenook**, **fake** it, wait until **last call** to get some, shower, trim, pine, **dress up** in a wrestling suit, tiptoe out of the house in stocking feet to avoid waking the **"last wo/man on Earth"** beside you, wonder "Where is this going?" Besides, if you don't love loving yourself, how can you expect anyone else to? It's Psych 101, people. Masturbation should always be your bit on the side, whether you haven't got laid in months or you're juggling two **booty call** partners and still finding time for the occasional **one-night stand** or you've finally decided to give **monogamy** a chance. Women: When you're having casual sex, your odds of getting off plummet, so it's especially important for you to know your coochie like the back of your hand. It

➔

can take a person *months* to figure out the best route to your particular happy place— so if you're going to keep them around for only a week or two, they'll need good directions. (Hint: They're more likely to take those directions if you gently guide them with oodles of positive reinforcement, rather than squealing, "Ouch! Not *there*, chump.") Plus, masturbation is a good way of, er, touching base with yourself. Sometimes you can get so caught up in the chase that you forget what actually feels nice. Masturbation always feels nice— and if it doesn't, you clearly need the practice. Men: Rubbing one out before you leave the house, à la *Something About Mary* (but with better aim), may significantly reduce your desperation level, which is especially key if you're still working on that whole master-of-**seduction** thing (see **economies of scale**). Masturbation is not a crime, kiddos, and it's not just for members of the geek patrol who are at least a decade away from getting laid, either.

ménage à trois

The French and/or pretentious term for a **three-way**.

mercy fuck

Sex with someone you are not particularly attracted to or don't necessarily want to do. You acquiesce simply because you feel sorry for them: Perhaps they've had a crush on you since sixth grade and swear they want "just one night of passion to help me move on," their pet goldfish just died, you know they'll be extra "giving" in the sack in return, you know this is your only hope of deprogramming them out of their cultish Trekkie community, their heart was just put through a blender (by you or someone else), they haven't had sex in a long time and have no prospects, they're dying of cancer, they're 30 years old and still a virgin. A.k.a. charity work (most often used as a negative rebuttal, as in "I don't *do* charity work." Oh, *snap*!). See also **breakup sex**, **comfort sex**, **grief therapy**.

metabolize

The process of getting an ex out of your system, usually endured by those who have been unceremoniously dumped: "It took me six months to metabolize that Jezebel." During the metabolism process, you may find yourself doing (m)any of the following: weeping openly on blind dates, dropping the name of your ex's favorite band name into casual conversation, leaving parties early to go home and check your email in case your ex has had a change of heart, being the drunkest at the party and the last to go home, **serial dating**, indulging in **heartbreak sex** with your **last wo/man on Earth**, annoying the shit out of your friends with your constant weeping, recoiling from **smug marrieds**, joining a gym, considering celibacy, taking up or quitting bad habits, **drunk dialing** high

school or college exes, drunk dialing your **mom**.

Method dating

Adopting the personality traits and beliefs of the person you are seeing, and in the process losing your sense of self. Especially annoying to your friends, who see you morph like a chameleon depending on who's standing by your side— i.e., just because you're **dating** *Jean-Claude* and he's taught you how to bake a goddamn soufflé, that doesn't give you the right to suddenly speak with a slight French accent! Who the hell do you think you are? Madonna? See also **tofu boyfriend/tofu girlfriend**.

metrosexual

The post-*Queer Eye* straight guy who prefers *Esquire* to *Maxim*, *GQ* to *Stuff*, and **Nerve** to *Playboy*. If you're a hetero girl, he's the boy you brought

→

home for Thanksgiving who your Dad pegged as gay, given the fabulous handmade cornucopia ice sculpture he brought. He gets his locks trimmed at a salon rather than a barber's and he knows more about waxing than you do. (Can you say "prepubescently bare balls"?) He'd quite like highlights if he could be sure his friends wouldn't rib him for it. He cooks gourmet meals for you and is horrified by the state of your toilet ("You don't own a toilet duck?"). IKEA is a four-letter word. At least one wall in his apartment is painted a color other than white. All his posters are framed, and none of them are of a band or a babe. He isn't afraid to admit he enjoys the finer, not to mention so-called girly, things in life. He'd like to be a **ladies' man**, but he likes his space too much. **Booty call** him once, though, and we guarantee he'll lure you into a little **intimacy lite**. Because, above all, metrosexuals like to be the inside spoon.

Mikey

❶ Someone who will try anything once. ❷ A narrow-minded poo-pooer so set in their ways that they're afraid of anything new or foreign, but who, when encouraged to try something new, actually enjoys it, despite their inclination not to. A prime example of this attitude is the sexist, homophobic, baseball cap-wearing frat boy who won't let his girlfriend anywhere near his **asshole** because "That's gay" but who actually turns out to love it one night when she sneakily administers a little back-door attention while giving him one of her "mind-blowing" *Cosmo* blow jobs, and who, against his better judgment, subsequently becomes a strap-on whore.

mile-high club

Being a member of it means you've fucked on a plane mid-flight. This experience has an inflated reputation–kind of like whipped cream, *9½ Weeks*, and sex in the shower. We have a feeling 95 percent of the people who do it, do it in order to say they've done it. Then again, the same could be said of **three-ways**, going to a **play party**, and rimming. But have you *seen* the size of the bathrooms on a JetBlue airplane? Maybe we'd understand the desire to fuck in transit if we flew first class more often. Yeah, yeah, it's taboo, you might get caught, blah, blah, blah. But couldn't you get the same thrill from wearing a butt plug for the seven-hour flight? And that way, you wouldn't have to let your bits and pieces touch any surface in an airborne loo (not to mention letting the line outside grow so long that it reaches the cockpit). If you must join this oh-so-exclusive club, try doing it in your seats, under a blanket, after all the cabin lights have been dimmed, the flight attendants have completed their duty-free rounds, and you've checked the vicinity for any underage passengers. But keep it down, would you? The rest of us are trying to enjoy our complimentary peanuts.

MILF

Acronym for "mother I'd like to fuck." It's not that there's anything inherently sexy about motherhood (at least as far as the young, single, childless guys who use the term are concerned); it's that our culture has traditionally assumed the experience of childbirth automatically renders a woman asexual. Therefore, to spot a

→

woman with a stroller *and* sex appeal is seemingly rare, and the idea of fucking her is taboo. The original MILF: Mrs. Robinson. Patron saints: Madonna, Liz Phair, Demi Moore, Cindy Crawford, Hillary Clinton. See also **virgin-whore complex**.

Missed Connections

A classifieds industry based entirely on people's blind (and unrealistic) faith in **romance**. It's a second chance to make a first move: You place an ad on **Craigslist** and in local alternative weeklies describing the guy in the khakis on the subway who didn't get off at your stop, the girl you talked to all night but lost on the dance floor before getting her **digits**, the aerobics instructor you fell in love with at first sight but were too chicken to approach—all on the off chance that they will read the Missed Connections section of the right paper on the right day and think you are their Mr./Mrs. Right, too. You have a better chance of being struck by lightning twice. Still, it's been known to happen: Our good friend Andra put an ad in her local alt weekly about the Steelers cap-wearing guy she locked eyes with in the **frozen food aisle** of her grocery store. Five years later, they're married and own a house together. Lucky bitch. A.k.a. I Saw You, Chance Meetings.

M

103

missionary position

Face-to-face sex (man-on-top, if you're hetero). *Do* assume the position if you're in love, you get off that way, it's **heartbreak sex** for both of you, you're making a baby, you're getting back together, you're filming a scene for a PG-rated movie. *Don't* assume the missionary position if you can't remember their name, it's **morning sex**, you're afraid of blurting out "I love you" (and it's a **one-night stand**), they're ugly.

modelizer

People who date/associate with models only: charming young men obsessed with outdoing their hetero friends; rich and/or famous middle-aged dudes desperately clinging to their youth; smart and rich but homely women who want to be beautiful by association and brilliant by comparison.

mom

❶ Someone you should call if you've just been dumped, you wake up hungover and lonely and convinced nobody is ever going to love you for *you*, you need first-date advice, you're in love, you're cooking dinner for a new crush, you haven't talked to her in over 2 weeks. Someone you shouldn't call if you need **booty call** guidance, you just got an **STD**, you're drunk. ❷ Someone you shouldn't mention during a **one-night stand** or a **booty call**. ❸ Someone who should be featured in photos on your fridge, *not* on your nightstand.

money shot

The climactic scene(s) in a pornographic movie in which the male star pulls out of some orifice so viewers can appreciate his ejaculate's color, texture, viscosity, inertia, force, distance, and impact. While you

→

may think it's cute to scream, "Show me the money . . . shot!" mid-**sesh**, it is not.

monogamy

It's natural, it's chemical (let's do it), it's logical, it's habitual (can we do it?), it's sensual, but, most of all, sex is something that we should do, sex is something for me and you, sex is natural, sex is good, not everybody does it, but everybody should. Sex is natural, sex is fun, sex is best when it's one on one. See also **Michael, George**.

moped

Someone who's fun to ride, though you wouldn't want to be seen with them in public.

morning sex

Sex at daybreak (or, if you're a freelancer, just before noon). It's not just for newlyweds: Some casual couplings feature it, too, especially during **appointment sex**, when you've grown comfortable enough with each other to do it sober. Fans of **intimacy lite** may dig it, too. And sometimes you wake up so freakin' glad you weren't wearing **beer goggles** the night before that you want to knock boots just to celebrate. If you're a **casual sex** aficionado who's comfortable with their body and doesn't need a buzz to feel like it's okay to enjoy sex for sex's sake, you may well expect it. Whatever your reason for doing it, we recommend **doggy style** or spoon sex over the **missionary position**—because even newlyweds and casual sex enthusiasts get morning breath.

mourning period (for the dumpee)

The time it takes you to **metabolize**, or get over, the fact that you will (probably) never have sex with a particular person again. Assuming this person was either the love of your life or the lay of your life, give yourself at least a week to hibernate, order in Chinese every night, not wash your hair, drink cheap wine in the afternoon, and watch a lot of romantic comedies and/or hardcore porn. Then begin the proactive healing process by getting in shape, helping the less fortunate in order to get some perspective on your petty **dating** probs, getting a haircut, engaging in **comfort sex**, **grief therapy**, **heartbreak sex**, **I-deserve-it sex**, or **I've-still-got-it sex**. This period should last approximately a month. If you have any pride, avoid **take-me-back sex** at all costs. If, after two months, you are confident in your personal fortitude, you may engage in **closure**. But be warned: Closure backfires more often than a Ford Pinto.

mourning period (for the dumper)

The time it takes you to **metabolize** someone whose heart you broke—probably, oh, two days. We're not saying you're a bad person; we're just saying that the wave of relief that comes with being the dumper (because, usually, you've put it off for at least a week, if not months) makes the whole thing a little easier to recover from. Sure, you might sob your heart out for 24 hours and wonder what the hell's wrong with you that you can't love anyone who loves you back. But the next morning, you'll spot a little honey on your morning commute and you'll bounce right back. It's a considerate gesture, however, to

→

observe a brief, seemly mourning period after a breakup. No one likes to see their heartbreaker back on the horse within hours, so have a bit of decorum when it comes to parading around town with someone new, and consider switching to a different online **dating** service and changing your username, too. If you're sure you can be discreet, go ahead and start slutting around town the next day. (And if you live in another state, screw the mourning period!) But for at least a month (more if it was a particularly traumatic breakup), avoid taking a date to places where your ex, or any close friends of your ex, are likely to see you. Stop whining: Would it kill you to give up eating lunch at Chili's for 8 weeks?

M

N

Nerve Personals

The **online personals** site affiliated with Nerve.com, the Web magazine about sex and pop culture. We used to work there and created the personals questionnaire with the now infamous field "_____ is sexy; _____ is sexier." (Yeah, sorry 'bout that.) Originally, since Nerve.com was known as literate smut, Nerve Personals gave people the illusion that they could be smart and sophisticated while trolling for sex (an oxymoron on **AdultFriendFinder.com**). When Nerve Personals got too big for its britches, Nerve.com spun it off into a separate technology company that syndicated the personals technology and user base to Web sites like Salon.com, TheOnion.com, and Esquire.com. (So when some hopelessly romantic bookworm signed up for Salon's personals, she tapped into *all* the network's users, including those who signed up with Nerve looking for cheap, meaningless, anonymous sex. Surprise!) In 2005, Nerve Personals was bought by FriendFinder (the company that owns AdultFriendFinder, natch). What was it that Elton John said about the circle of life?

nice-guy syndrome

The myth that nice guys can't get laid. Just as penis envy is something men *wish* women had, NGS is something losers *wish* they suffered from. The socially awkward, the fatally shy, and the victims of halitosis all like to use NGS as an excuse for their poor **sack record**, instead of taking a cold, hard look at their own self-sabotage. It's their way of avoiding the hard work of personal growth and change required to improve their **body count**. Men: Don't mistake neediness, spinelessness, and a stutter for niceness; women certainly don't. Being nice means being considerate, honest, and sincere—and that's hot. If a woman tells you, "You're just too nice," she's either too nice herself to tell you the *real* reason she doesn't want to date you, or she's a self-hating psycho who dates only **assholes** and has more issues than *TV Guide*. Those who fall into this latter category are best left alone until they grow up or get therapy. Real women fuck nice guys. See also **economies of scale**, **pickup artists**.

nookie

A so-cute-you-could-puke term for sex. It rhymes with *cookie*, so what do you expect?

nooner

❶ Sex at or around noon on a workday: You leave your respective (and probably respectable) daytime jobs to meet at a sleazy motel for some lunch-break **nookie**. Would you like fries with that? ❷ Midday sex with a coworker in an empty, locked conference room, typically arranged over **IM** (look, Ma, no record!) after a particularly rousing PowerPoint presentation. ❸ Locking yourself in a bathroom stall and rubbing one out in the middle of a tough day at the office.

note

❶ What good manners dictate you leave if you abscond before your **one-night stand**, **booty call**, or partner wakes up. You may scribble, "You were great last night" or leave a twenty-dollar bill on the nightstand, but only if you're sure your partner will appreciate the ironic joke (in other words, you may not leave either one sincerely). Your phone number and "I'd love to see you again" will suffice, if you do in fact wish to see them again. If not, try a simple "I hate to come and run, but work calls. I had a fantastic time. Take care!" The "Take care!" is polite code for "Have a nice life!" See also **Post-it note.** ❷ An ironic way to make a pass at someone in a crowded **bar**. It's endearing because it recalls the sweet, innocent **romance** of junior high. Bonus points for including boxes the recipient may check off, as in, "Can I buy you a drink?: _ Yes _ No _ Maybe" or "Would you care to dance?: _ Why, yes, I'd be delighted _ Maybe after you buy me another drink _ No thank you, I don't have rhythm."

nudie pics

Amateur porn by People Like Us—i.e., submissions to *Hustler*'s "Beaver Hunt" don't count. We don't understand hipster knitting circles and bingo nights—don't you guys want to save *something* for later? You'll have plenty of time for all those golden-oldie hobbies when you're 83 years old with a blue rinse or a blue pill. Stop the golfing, the crocheting, the cookie baking, and the scrapbooking, and do something you *can't* save for later—take nudie pics (a.k.a. X-rated scrapbooking)! Important note: During casual **hookups**, the only kind of nudie pics we can, in good faith, recommend are either Polaroids (where each party must approve who keeps which pics, and which pics will be destroyed on the spot) or digital (where each party has a say in which pics get deleted on the spot)—in both cases, keeping only those shots without identifying characteristics like, oh, say, your face. And don't take their word for it that the incriminating pics are deleted, 'cause you just *know* your **booty call** would rather show their friends dirty pics of you than honor your modest requests. You may not give a shit right now, but what if you want to star in a reality-TV series 5 years from now, and your ex-**booty call** decides to sell those dirty pics to the

→

National Enquirer? (Doesn't your great-aunt read the *Enquirer?*) If your concerns have less to do with privacy than with aesthetics, spend some time browsing amateur porn online: You've got a better eye than you think. Check out what works ("candid" shots, cheeky shots with a sense of humor, mood lighting, shooting from above) and what definitely doesn't (overhead lighting, shooting from below, close-up beaver shots, harsh flashbulbs, floral couches). Strike poses that flatter. In Polaroids (again, no negs!), everyone looks good or at least a little bit arty. And don't feel pressure to go gonzo; sometimes the sexiest shots are about what's suggested instead of what's explicitly shown. Delete or destroy as you go—in fact, you may end up keeping none of the pics. Often, the best part is pointing the camera at each other while you do it, then huddling over the preview screen to check out the results. So what if the pics exist for only one evening, for a very private viewing for two? It's the ultimate in exclusivity, and, as Paris Hilton would say, that's hot. On a final note, just in case your mama didn't raise you right: Even if you're taking only PG-13-rated pics, make sure everyone involved is over 18; never take a nudie pic while someone is asleep or while they're tied up and blindfolded (unless you ask nicely first), and never take a snapshot of her wet spot while she's using the bathroom so you can prove to your buddies that you made her ejaculate like a porn star.

o

occasion sex

❶ Sex that's hot due to circumstance—you could hump in the missionary position for 2 minutes, but if it's during a power outage, it'll feel like the first time. Occasion sex may be celebratory (first anniversary, you just decided to make a baby, Hillary Clinton wins the presidential election, you win the lottery, good hair day) or commiserative (Ah-nold wins the presidential election after a constitutional amendment qualifies him, death of a pet, bad haircut). ❷ Sudden, temporary increase in **one-night stands** and **casual sex** across the country due to a power outage, a heat wave, an announcement of war, a notification that the terror alert has been raised to orange, a new Al Green album.

off limits

Someone you may never, *ever* sleep with: the guy or girl who broke your best friend's/sibling's/parent's heart, the ex who's still madly in love with you and who begged you to stop **booty calling** them because they can't say no, someone who reports to you at work (have them moved to a different department if you can't keep your hands on your own mouse), anyone who's in a monogamous relationship *with someone else*, anyone who refuses to wear protection, anyone who insists on wearing a baseball cap at the dinner table.

office holiday party

An annual party thrown a week or two before Christmas by one's corporate employers that's accidentally yet invariably more debauched than a long weekend at Hedonism II. The majority of employees

→

will get drunk like they did in college, two people who hate each other *will* make out under the mistletoe (if not fuck the shit out of each other in the stairwell; see **hate fucking**), and someone *will* **Xerox** their butt cheeks.

One Leg Up

The members-only **group-sex** parties in New York City that prompted every magazine, newspaper, alt weekly, and its brother to "report" the widespread, national "comeback" of the **orgy**. Please—it never went away. Visit www.onelegupnyc.com for more details, or just watch reruns of HBO's *Real Sex*.

one-night stand

One-time-only sex with someone, usually mere hours after the "nice to meet you." Before all else: Have you signed your **prenook**? Okay, now we can get to the fun part. Actually, maybe not just yet. Because it has come to our attention that some of you consider the following activities to be appropriate **foreplay** during a one-night stand: drawing a bubble bath in a candlelit bathroom, bringing out your thesis or poetry chapbook, playing love songs on your guitar. A one-night stand is too fleeting and flimsy to bear the weight of such romance-laden activities—save those for your monogamous partner, who has no choice but to listen to your "modern take" on Extreme's "More Than Words." Besides, if one of these aforementioned activities is your one-night shtick, you *will* earn a nickname like "e. e. *cum*mings," and you *will* get busted when you repeat yourself a month later with someone who happens to be a distant relative of your April **hookup**. A one-night stand is about the **commitment**-free bumping of latex-protected uglies—nothing more, nothing less. Make the sex dirty, your manners immaculate, your

baggage light, and the mood breezy and cheery. Don't talk about any prescription drugs you may be hooked on or what your therapist thinks of **casual sex**; *do* talk about your sexual history as it relates to the risks involved with the sex you're about to have. Don't talk about their appearance if you've got nothing nice to say—even if *you* think your comment is "neutral." Trust us; it won't come off that way, and nobody likes to be told, "You've got funny boobs" or "I've never seen an erection curve like that." When it comes to the sex, don't sulk if you don't get everything you asked Santa for—only people in relationships are allowed to complain when things don't go their way in bed (and even then they should stop focusing on the negative and just be grateful someone puts up with them). Finally, if you lure someone back to your place in the sticks, offer them a ride home—and take them all the way, damn it. We don't care if you're late for work: Dropping her off at 7 A.M. in the center of town so she can catch a bus home in her party frock and four-inch heels is poor form. And if your one-night stand is late for work, you're not allowed to hide his shoes so he'll be forced to stick around for **morning sex** (though you should feel free to do this to your regular **booty call**). See also **about last night**, **bondage**, **booty buzz**, **deal breaker**, **doggy style**, **faking**, **hickey**, **home-team advantage**, **hosting**, **humor**, **"I'll call you,"** **intimacy lite**, **jumping the shark**, **last call**, **mom**, **missionary position**, **occasion sex**, **oral sex**, **safe(r) sex**.

online personals

Internet profiles posted by individuals to announce their search for a soul mate, a prom date, or a **pinch hitter**. Online **dating** has created **casual sex** opps for those too shy, too sober, too tongue tied, too busy, too old, or too "over that whole scene" to **close the deal** at

→

last call. Unfortunately, online dating has also opened up **adultery** to the lily-livered, would-be-unfaithful masses—those too afraid of being caught, too bald, or too homebound to attempt it the old-fashioned way. Infidelity aside, we wish everyone would just get over the so-called stigma of online dating. Unlike the **classifieds**, it's not a last resort for lonely hearts and social outcasts; it's just a way to expand your circle beyond the **bar**. (Like it's soooo "romantic" to meet someone at a club after four dirty martinis, when your speech is slurred, your breath is rancid, and you're standing only thanks to a very sturdy bar stool. If that's "fate" or Cupid at work, we'll risk the odds and go it alone, thank you very much.) Seriously, what are you waiting for? Have an artsy friend snap some flattering pics of you (not *too* flattering, mind you; you don't want to disappoint your blind dates), have a witty friend help you write a charming paragraph or two (with *no* mention of **oral sex** prowess), and

have a friend with too much time on their hands help you vet the candidates. All we ask is that you not lie in your ad—not about your height, weight, age, or what you're looking for (be it friendship, dating, a soul mate, or "**play**"). Don't sit back and wait for the hotties to come to you: Get out there and respond to every ad that catches your eye, or at least add it to your Favorites list—think **economies of scale**. As in any pickup scene, you'll have to wade through your share of undesirables, but, with patience and determination, a like-minded individual is sure to be found. (Hey, if the **Internet** can bring a cannibal and a dude with a death wish together, it can work for you, too!) Once you've established a connection over email (this should take no more than a week or five emails apiece, whichever comes first), arrange to meet up for one drink or one **coffee**—anything more is too much of a time investment in someone whose pheromones you have yet to inhale. But remember:

➜

It's their time investment, too, so turn up on time, for manners' sake. Once there, even if there's no chemistry, you're nonetheless obliged to a) stay for 45 minutes—and no having a friend "stop by" to save you—and b) offer your undivided attention for those 45 minutes (unless of course they *grossly* misled you as to their age/weight/gender or they show up wearing a cape). You're *not* obliged to give your blind date any kind of carnal loving—not even a cheek kiss—even if you arranged to **play**, even if you negotiated a comprehensive **prenook** over email, even if the IM-ing got so hot you actually came in your pants at your office computer. See also **AdultFriendFinder.com**, **Craigslist**, **Nerve Personals**.

open relationship

A relationship between two highly evolved people—i.e., they're missing the **jealousy** gene—who are in love (whatever that means) but who jointly agree to forgo convention and have **casual sex** with other people. (BTW: A relationship in which one or both people are secretly cheating on the other does not count as an open relationship.) This kind of setup is based on the idea that human beings aren't wired to be monogamous, that love can and should be separated from sex, that you can never own or control another person, and that the sixties were way cool, man. Every open relationship is different and requires explicit negotiation between the two parties in order to determine their particular **rules**—some couples may be cool with **out-of-towners** only, while others may invite third parties to join them in the bedroom every third Saturday of the month. See also **polyamory**.

oral sex

❶ Lustful or loving mouth-to-genital contact that evolved

→

types realize *is* sex, though it is still favored as a "doesn't-count" substitute by teens, presidents, and Park Avenue princesses fixated on their **body count**. Though teen (and even tween) girls nowadays seem happy to put their mouths on anything with a frenulum, many *adult* women find oral sex too intimate for a **one-night stand**, so don't force it. Guys: Don't say "Suck me" while pushing your partner's head down like it's a toilet plunger, and don't force *your* way down, either, while announcing, "Trust me, it'll be the best you ever had." (In fact, don't *ever* say, "Trust me, it'll be the best you ever had.") Ladies, this all goes for you, too: Don't be pushing your partner's head down and commanding them to "Suck it" unless you know for sure they dig your diva attitude, or you're role-playing that "Ivana and her pool boy" scenario again. If your partner wants to be a giver, they'll find their own way downtown. Asking is tacky, and begging is beneath you.

❷ Something you should never, *ever* mention in your **online personals** ad (unless you're on **AdultFriendFinder.com**). Those who talk the talk rarely walk the walk. Let your oral acumen speak for itself when the time comes (as it were). See also **bases**, **facial**, **safe(r) sex**.

orgasms

What men hope to get out of **rec sex**. Women, on the other hand, hope to get self-esteem, validation of their sexiness, sensuality, an **ego boost**, an adrenaline rush, adventure, romance, mystery—you name it. It usually takes more time than rec sex allows for a **casual sex** partner to find the road to a woman's happy place, so orgasms are low on her rec sex priority list. However, there *is* the rare bird who *requires* the excitement of rec sex and its attendant **booty buzz** in order to reach orgasm. Her name is Tanya; be nice to her, because she's had a rough life.

orgy

More commonly referred to as a "**play party**" these days, an orgy is a party where everybody gets off *before* **last call** (though there's rarely a money-back guarantee). Some orgies are more organized than a Mensa convention (see **One Leg Up**), and others are spontaneous eruptions of lust, especially at after-parties featuring cocaine or ecstasy and lots of **BUTs**. An organized play party makes a perfect **booty call** date, as you've allegedly already tackled the **jealousy** issue and have banished the concepts of ownership and **monogamy**. And if you're jaded about the pickup scene at **bars** (maybe your proposal of cheap, easy, no-strings-attached sex didn't go down so well in the Regal Beagle), orgies are the place for you. Men should be forewarned, though, that they'll need a female plus-one to get into most organized het orgies—at least, those worth attending. Try trawling **Nerve Personals** (if you live in NYC) or **AdultFriendFinder.com** (if you live anywhere else) for a willing companion. Like the **mile-high club**, orgies always sound much more fun than they actually are. At least, that's what we keep telling ourselves. See also **cuddle party**, **group sex**, **safe(r) sex**, **three-way**.

O

out-of-towner

❶ A **booty call** who resides in a separate state, allowing the two of you to continue the sordid state of affairs for many months—even years, if a plane journey divides you. Out-of-towners are more likely to have **bounce** than the average **booty call**. See also **rain check**. ❷ Cheating on your partner while on a business trip—or, worse, traveling to meet your booty call and telling your partner you're out of town on business. See **adultery** for our emphatic position on this. ❸ In some **open relationships**, couples will make a rule that they are to be monogamous on home ground, but out-of-town **nookie** is allowed. See also **layaway**.

outercourse

Term applied to hetero and gay-male relations, in which sexual activity includes anything *except* penile penetration. People engage in outercourse for various reasons: They want to hold onto their V-card, they don't want to increase their total **body count**, they want to reduce their **STD** risk (see **body-fluid monogamy**), they're suffering from **[blank] dick**, they don't want to be taken for a **slut**, they don't want to lose **hand**. A.k.a. everything but sex (EBS). See also **hooking up**.

o

P

palate cleanser

❶ **Rebound** sex that obliterates the bad taste left in your mouth (*not* literally) by a recent ex. A.k.a. sorbet sex. ❷ Term of endearment you use with your friends to describe the person with whom you had palate-cleansing sex.

park, to

Archaic term referring to the still common teenage practice of driving somewhere with a decent amount of privacy—a dead end, an office parking lot, an automated car wash (**quickies** only), or Make-out Point—to, *duh*, make out. Not to be confused with **dogging**.

party favor

❶ Someone you take home from a party or a night out—not because your eyes meet across a crowded room and you're drawn to each other like peanut butter to chocolate, but simply because you dressed for sex (see **lucky underwear**) and you're damned if you're going to go home alone tonight. ❷ A **casual sex** blind date or setup. A matchmaking friend who likes to force their single friends to mingle may make certain introductions simply because it's been a while since either of them got some. This kind of party favor is most often extended when one has an out-of-town friend visiting for the weekend, especially in college or soon thereafter. Let's say your best friend just got dumped and is in sore need of a **palate cleanser**. And let's say your college roommate's rugby teammate is ideally suited for the role. Add liquor,

→

shake well on the dance floor, and remove condom from wrapper before heating. See also **proxy**.

phoner

Phone sex with someone you've never met (and perhaps have no intention of ever meeting), either because you randomly dialed a number and somehow got the person on the other end of the line to reciprocate the **dirty talk**, you were randomly rung up and liked what you heard, or you met online. Once you've met in person, it's just plain phone sex. If one of you is a decidedly unwilling (or even unwitting) participant, it's not a phoner—it's a crime (and if it's not, it should be). And if one of you has to give up a credit card number first, it's not a phoner; it's just a little sad. Some people actually seek out phoners, while others merely stumble on

them: They just can't resist responding to the ad of that hottie living halfway around the world, and, before they know it, they're steaming up the international lines on a regular basis. And why not? It's like conjuring a fantasy and having them talk back to you—and talk back *dirty* to you. It's 100 percent safe sex, and sometimes it's just nice to have company while you rub one out. As for the **booty buzz** you'll get off a phoner, dig it: You'll be washing your mouth out with soap every night!

P

phoning it in

Perfunctory fucking. The onset of **ennui** doesn't always mean the end of **casual sex**. You may find yourself taking **booty calls** or going through the motions of a **one-night stand** simply out of habit. The sex will be unremarkable, as will your performance. You know those nights when you drink like a fish but go straight to drowsy and hungover without ever feeling a buzz? Phoning it in is like that, but with sex. A.k.a. a boregasm.

pickup artists (PUAs)

A network of het male geeks who have turned the art of seduction into a science, employing techniques of **hypnosis**, magic tricks, and mind control to—they claim—*guarantee* sexual success with the ladies. With one of the leading pickup gurus (and there are many) boasting a mailing list 2 million strong and growing, this secret society isn't exactly small. And with the recent publication of a book exposing the inner workings of the community (*The Game* by Neil Strauss), it's not really secret anymore. By far the best part of the exposé is the list of "negs," or subtle insults, that PUAs recommend to chip away at a woman's self-confidence and thus make her more needy for your approval, such as, "Those shoes look really comfortable"; "That's a nice skirt; I see a lot of girls wearing it these days"; and, our favorite, "You kinda have man hands." See also **nice-guy syndrome**, **pickup lines**.

pickup lines

Booty gambits. Please don't tell us people are *still* initiating conversations with "Come here often?" and "What's your sign?" and "Is your father a thief?" in the hopes of getting laid. How many times do we have to say this: Introduce yourself, ask

→

someone to dance, offer to buy a drink—and that's it. If you can come up with something truly original, go for it. (If *we* gave you a line, it wouldn't be original, now, would it?) But if you've used the line before or you're lying, we'd throw up a red flag. If he really *does* remind you of someone you've met before, feel free to tell him so. If she really *does* have lovely eyes, wait at least 15 minutes before mentioning it. Compliments are like lightsabers—they must be wielded wisely, honestly, and for the greater good, Luke. Don't be the Darth Vader of the pickup scene. See also **clichés**, **pickup artists**.

pinch hitter

A substitute sex partner. This could be a **palate cleanser** after a breakup, a **booty call** you rely on during dry spells, or a third party you invite for a **ménage à trois**, etc. The pinch hitter is not someone you want around all the time—just occasionally will

do, when you're in desperate need of some kink. If your sexual desires are a team, the pinch hitter is a genuine **team player**. A.k.a. **Sextra**.

play

If there's no sandbox involved and no one's riding a banana-seat bike, it's a whole different kind of play: the *adult* kind. It's seriously naughty sex without all that **dating**, from **three-ways** to **one-night stands** to **booty calls**—the closest thing to **free love** the twenty-first century has seen. The term is used most often in **online personals**, especially the **Nerve Personals**, **Craigslist**, and any sites with the word *adult* or *gay* in their title. If someone is "seeking play," according to their personal ad, it's typically not 15 minutes of noncommittal missionary they're after. Nope, play is sex with an action plan: It's frequently creative, exploratory, and a wee bit kinky. And if it's not, why are

P

you bothering? There's plenty of uncreative sex out there to be had, with people who frown on the very concept of sex outside of a relationship. (Not that a relationship makes it impossible to have creative, kinky sex—but then it's not play; it's just cool.) Once you've jumped that sex-minus-a-relationship hurdle together and left societal expectations behind, why *not* celebrate with a little light spanking, a bout of role-playing, or a round of naked Trivial Pursuit?

play d'oh!

A **casual sex** blooper. A few of our favorites: Bleating "I love you" on a **one-night stand**, right as you come; crying right after you come (especially common after **heartbreak sex**); accidentally **drunk dialing** your boss's cell phone instead of your ex's—and tuning out during the recorded message so you end up leaving your boss a voicemail to remember; wearing that pair of undies with the skid mark because you're "only stopping by the **bar** for one quick drink," and ending up in bed with a beautiful stranger; forgetting someone's name at the exact moment they moan, "Say my name"; wiping so thoroughly right before a **hookup** that you leave a teeny wad of TP wedged in your crack.

play party

A modern-day **orgy** organized by someone with a degree in event planning. See **orgy** for a more in-depth definition, then see **group sex** for more supplemental info, then see **One Leg Up** for an example, and then stop whining about all the flipping you have to do—this is a sexual adventure!

playa

A **player** who wears gold chains, listens to Eminem, uses those annoying Nextel

→

walkie-talkies, and speaks with a ghetto-fabulous accent, even though they were born in Fargo, North Dakota.

playa-hata (*alt.*: player-hater)

❶ Someone who finds the player MO reprehensible and actively tries to undermine a player's rap. The patron saint of playa-hatas has got to be Terrifica, a turn-of-the-century thirty-something superhero in a blond Brunhilde wig, a gold mask, a Valkyrie bra, and a red cape. Terrifica can be seen prowling the **bars** of New York City in search of drunk girls to save from the paws of **players**. (We're not making this up.) ❷ A feminist. ❸ Someone who's insanely jealous of players because they themselves couldn't get laid at a Hawaiian luau.

playdar

The **casual sex** equivalent of **gaydar**: When your sixth sense tells you that the person you're dry humping on the dance floor will be more than amenable to your dirty suggestion, whether that's being a **pinch hitter**, dressing up in a leotard and leg warmers and riding you like a balance beam, or simply coming back to your place and going "all the way" (see **bases**). Playdar does not make a **prenook** moot, though it will improve your odds of receiving a favorable response to this prenook.

player

A person (typically male) who gets a lot of action, usually through dubious means, like pretending he really likes you, taking advantage of you when you're drunk, telling you he has only three months to live. A.k.a. Lothario (the foppish, unscrupulous rake from Nicholas Rowe's 1703 tragedy *The Fair Penitent*).

P

pleated pants

Threads to avoid if you want to get lucky.

plot spoiler

❶ Three inches of thong poking out of the top of your lo-rise jeans. See also **lucky underwear**. ❷ Sexual braggadocio on a first date. Come to think of it: sexual braggadocio, period. ❸ Coming in her hand as she unzips your fly (rare after junior high).

polyamory

Long-term sexual and romantic relationships among multiple partners who usually sport one or more of the following: a sensitive ponytail, facial hair, tie-dyed attire, Tevas, an Enya collection, crystal necklaces, pot growing in their bathroom. Unlike **players** or participants in an occasional **three-way**, polyamorists are committed to each other, but not in some possessive, controlling, manipulative way, man. They are all about the open, honest, and painfully earnest expression of their love. Not to be confused with polygamists, who are scary religious men with multiple teenage wives-slash-baby factories. Polyamorists, on the other hand (and there are plenty of other hands), are laid back, egalitarian, and often bisexual. They may live together, like in a big adobe house in Santa Fe. While people in **open relationships** may share polyamorists' rejection of jealousy, the former are much more stylish.

Post-it note

A self-adhesive yellow piece of paper perfect for leaving a postcoital "Thanks for the hot monkey lovin'!" **note** on the nightstand. Or, if the note says something überdirty, like, "Next time, *I* get to hold the ice cream scooper"—i.e., something that couldn't possibly be misconstrued as romantic— it may be stuck to their pillow. Convenient for leaving a "Honey, don't forget to pick up more lube" note on the fridge. Not at all appropriate for leaving a "Dear John" note (as most of us learned from that *Sex and the City* episode).

Call Cindy and John about tonight's spouse swap

posterity poke

Sex intended to make a baby. Not usually seen in the area of **casual sex**, except where surrogates are concerned (can you say "awkward"?). A.k.a. reproduction.

prenook

Casual sex equivalent of the prenup. The prenook is more about honest communication than about the literal presence of a fifteen-page signed document—it verbally outlines both parties' intentions and **sexpectations**. If you have absolutely zero interest in seeing someone again, it would be wrong to lure them home with promises (even implicit promises) of a beautiful relationship. And if you think your **booty call** partner is just hanging in there in the hope of converting you into a boyfriend or girlfriend, you must retire that booty call number ASAP. There is no one-size-fits-all

P

→

pronouncement that secures a prenook—after all, "Let's have a **one-night stand**" or "Is it okay if I never call you again?" will kill the mood for most people (though either of these lines might work if spoken with the right dose of **humor**). A prenook is kind of like porn: You know it when you see it. In certain sexed-up circumstances (say, spring break in Cancun, or a swingers' convention in Tampa), the prenook goes without saying. At times like these, the implicit promise is that you *will* get laid, and you *will* get laid *tonight*. Therefore, a spring break prenook operates in reverse: a) You must fess up before getting to the bedroom if you suffer from erectile dysfunction, and b) you must provide a heads-up if all you're in for is a kiss and a cuddle (though it goes without saying that anyone can change their minds as to how far they are willing to go at any point—we're talking to you, date rapers). The reverse prenook allows the recipient to look for their jollies elsewhere, should they so desire.

primer

Primer? I hardly know her! But seriously, folks, primer is nonsexual foreplay with someone you have yet to bed. It's different from **game playing** because you're not doing it to gain **hand**—a primer coat is simply delayed gratification. It's not **dating**, and it's never planned: It's just casual hanging out as a result of sharing a local **bar**/circle of friends/ bowling league. In **casual sex**, the chase is at least half the fun, so why not draw it out over a few evenings? Talk all night at a bar, but don't ask for his **digits** (that's what **Friendster** research is for); make out for hours on her stoop and then catch a bus home to your own place; take someone back to your place for a **dry run**. Quaint, we know. It's kind of like fifties courtship, except you both know that what's coming is not the exchange of class rings, but, rather, wake-the-neighbors, **commitment**-free copulation.

proxy

❶ The next-best thing to a certain kind of sex, which often turns out to be better than the "best" thing: Maybe you and your partner get off on the idea of a **three-way**, but you just can't see yourselves actually picking up a **pinch hitter**, much less having breakfast with them the following morning. Or maybe you fear the after-shock of attending a **play party** together–especially if you recently rented *Indecent Proposal* together and fought over whether Demi should have slept with Robert Redford. So, instead, you meet a hottie of an unidentifiable sexual orientation at a party and tag-team flirt with them, all the while making eyes at each other. Maybe you sneak off to the bathroom together for some heavy petting before rejoining the group. In the cab on the way home, you talk about what might have happened if you'd asked the pinch hitter to join you. You keep talking–all the way into the bedroom. That's what we call a proxy **three-way**: no rejection, no jealousy, no **rules**, no awkward breakfasts. ❷ Do you ever meet someone and think, "I would be going home with them tonight if I wasn't so old or so married or so close with their heartbroken ex"? Do you then use matchmaking as an excuse to flirt with them, and work hard to ensure that a well-deserving, not to mention loose-lipped, friend of yours takes this person home as a **party favor**? And do you invite said loose-lipped friend to brunch the following morning to hear all the sordid details? You just **pulled** by proxy. See also **brunch story**.

pull, to (British)

To **score** more than **digits**.

Q

quality control

A system for ensuring the maintenance of proper standards in casual sex, especially by periodic random inspection of the act by concerned sexually active singles. Self-appointed quality control officers carry their own fresh condoms at all times, insist on seeing HIV-test results before bodily fluids are dabbled in, never *ever* fake orgasm, and give gentle yet constructive advice (for example, to bad kissers or girls who literally blow on the penis).

quarterlife crisis

❶ Familiarly, the utter horror a twenty-something experiences when ejected from the structured world of academia into the unstructured world of reality without a clue about how to rent an apartment, cook a meal, or find a decent job. (See *Get It Together: Surviving Your Quarterlife Crisis* by Damian Barr and *Conquering Your Quarterlife Crisis* by Alexandra Robbins.) ❷ As it applies to **rec sex**: The utter horror a twenty-something experiences when ejected from the contained dating pool of one's cute, young, like-minded peers into the huge and scary dating world of psychos, liars, and leches without a clue about how to obtain health insurance that covers birth control, write a decent personal ad, or arrange a date that doesn't involve keg stands.

quickie

Sex that purposefully takes less than 10 minutes. (Sorry, folks, sex involving premature ejaculation doesn't count.) Of course, if you're **Sting**, a quickie could take an hour and a half. It usually happens spontaneously and impulsively, when you're late for some event or when your

➔

relatives are about to arrive for dinner. Often cited in women's mags as an easy way to "spice things up," the quickie is best suited for long-term couples who need a pinch of chili powder and/or who know how to get each other off in record time. New or **casual sex** partners should relish long **seshes** and take their time getting to know each other's bodies, because the newness *is* the spice.

quirkyalone

The opposite of a **serial dater**. A quirkyalone is a **singleton** without the self-image problem, someone who actually enjoys being single. According to QuirkyAlone.net, a QA isn't against relationships in principle, but they aren't going to date just for the sake of having someone to slow-dance with at weddings. In other words, a QA is a well-adjusted **slut**. Put a bunch of quirkyalones together and you get an **urban tribe**.

R

rain check

A promise that an unclaimed offer of sex will be valid at a future date. For instance, you may **booty call** a **friend with benefits**, only to find out that they just decided to give **monogamy** a try with a new partner, so you offer them a rain check for future no-strings-attached boot knocking if (when) this whole **commitment** thing doesn't work out for them. (Don't expect to get invited to the wedding if it does.) See also **bounce, out-of-towner**.

rebound

Sex with someone new after a breakup. This umbrella term covers **heartbreak sex** and **palate cleansers**, and may also sometimes include **grief therapy, I-deserve-it-sex**, and **I've-still-got-it sex**. If you're fucking on the rebound, it's always sex with a qualifying adjective.

rec sex

Joy riding, wherein you are happily being ridden or are happily riding someone else. Short for "recreational sex," this kind of fucking for the fun of it usually comes from a positive, happy place; in other words, if you were depressed or heartbroken or enraged, the sex you had shouldn't officially be called rec sex. But, really, any sex between two or more consenting adults outside of a long-term relationship could be referred to as rec sex. And rec sex doesn't ensure that there won't be any negative *consequences* (like heartbreak, **jealousy**, confusion, or **STDs**). But while you're doing it, you're not worried about the future: You're in the moment. Rec sex is often employed as a more cheery synonym for **casual sex**, and is particularly common after one has sold a first novel, won the lottery, or received a tax refund. See also the introduction to this book.

reciprocation

Scratching the back of someone who just scratched yours, when "back scratching" is a euphemism for "giving someone an earth-shattering orgasm." Many young **luvvas** erroneously assume that the nature of **casual sex** allows them to forgo reciprocation and act purely selfishly—i.e., thrust/rub, come, roll over, sleep. However, anyone doing you the favor of lending you their body for your pleasure certainly deserves a little one-way sexual attention in return. It's just good manners, not to mention good **karma**.

reference check

Getting a second opinion (yours being the first) about someone you're considering sleeping with. Perhaps when you met this person, you were wearing **beer goggles** or were simply blinded by lust due to a six-month dry spell. So you call on a friend who moves in this candidate's circle, you **google** this person's name, or you secretly follow them home one evening after work, all in the hopes of determining whether they are married/subscribe to *Soldier of Fortune*/are on a day-release program (all potential **deal breakers**, one would hope). See also **dry run**.

Rejection Hotline

One of the twenty-first century's greatest inventions: local telephone numbers in just about every major American city that, when called, play a recorded message explaining that the person who gave you this number did not want you to have their real **digits**, for any number of reasons: You're not their type, you have bad breath, you give off that creepy, psycho-stalker vibe, or you seem "as appealing as playing leap frog with unicorns" (that's a direct quote!). The Web site, RejectionHotline.com,

→

argues that this is a genuine public service: "The rejector has an easy way to get rid of unwanted suitors, to express a lack of interest in a nonconfrontational manner, and to gracefully escape an uncomfortable situation. The rejectee, on the other hand, is able to hear the bad news in the privacy of his/her own home without being subjected to the embarrassment and/or ridicule of a more public rejection. Furthermore, there are no unanswered 'what ifs,' no desperate assumptions of 'I must have just misdialed,' and no ambiguity—all of which are common by-products of the randomly selected fake numbers which were more common before the advent of the Rejection Hotline." See also **faux no**.

reputation

❶ What Rizzo had in *Grease*. But we happen to agree that there *are* worse things she could do than go with a boy or two—like lie, cheat, steal, or watch Fox News, for example. See also **tease**. ❷ In a fair and just world, what you'd get if you slutted around town, **prenooks** be damned, leaving a trail of broken hearts in your wake. ❸ In an unfair and unjust world—that'd be this one—what a woman gets if she enjoys sex for sex's sake, *especially* if she pays attention to the niceties of a prenook. See also **double standard**, **glass ceiling**, **slut**.

retrosexual

A person who fucks like they are living in the fifties. Unlike funky old martini-maker sets and Elvis (the young version), retrosexuals are *not* cool. They make at least one of the following assumptions: Men always pay for the date, sex before marriage is a sin (unless you're a man), women don't enjoy sex (or don't need to), a clitoral orgasm is a poor man's vaginal orgasm (à la Freud), homosexuality is a disease, **foreplay** lasts approximately 10.5 seconds, and women's sexual responsibilities include cooking, cleaning, and foot massaging.

returning to the well

Sex with a previous partner, usually because they're easy and you're lazy. A.k.a. double dipping, ex sex, blue binning, recycling.

reunion

❶ A get-together of high school classmates 5, 10, or 20 years after graduation, where you can (and most likely will) make out on the dance floor with the former captain of your football team/cheerleading squad, the one who never gave you a second look back then, and who is now at least one of the following: divorced, bloated, bald, depressed, living down the street from your parents, out on parole for good behavior. ❷ A get-together of college classmates 5, 10, or 20 years after graduation where you can (and probably will) sleep with your ex and show off all your new moves. ❸ A get-together of extended family members, where you can (but hopefully won't) finger your hot second cousin.

revenge sex

❶ A specific sex act intended to inflict punishment in return for some emotional, physical, or financial injury. Let's say your business partner cheated you out of your share of the profits, so you seduce their spouse, take pictures of the act with a hidden camera, and feature the pics in the company newsletter—that's revenge sex.

R

Or imagine that your high school boyfriend dumped you because you were "too fat," so 10 years later at the **reunion**, after training at Bally's and running the Iron Man, you take his flabby ass back to your hotel room, get him worked up, make him strip, and point and laugh at his dinky winky—that's revenge sex. (This happens more in people's vivid imaginations and on daytime television than in reality.) ❷ A subconscious sexual MO based on some past hurt. Meg Ryan, in *When Harry Met Sally*, nails it when she responds to Billy Crystal's insistence that she get laid to get over her ex: "What the hell does that have to do with anything? That will prove I'm over Joe? Because I *fuck* somebody? Harry, you're gonna have to move back to New Jersey, because you've slept with everybody in New York, and I don't see that turning [your ex-wife] into a faint memory for you. Besides, I will make love to somebody when it is *making love*. Not the way you do it,

like you're out for revenge or something." We'll have what she's having! A.k.a. sex with a vengeance. See also **hate fucking**, **roger dodger**.

ring finger

The digit on the left hand that's next to the pinkie—memorize this, people! Look for a band of metal or an untanned and slightly indented band of skin. If he claims he's in an **open relationship**, you should go back to his room anyway and ask him who wrote *The Ethical Slut.* If he's never heard of it, he's probably lying like a dog. If *she* says she's in an open relationship, she's probably telling the truth. Married men of our acquaintance swear that their wedding band is a 24-karat **aphrodisiac** to single ladies, but we think most of those women just enjoy flirting when they know it can't lead to anything. As for the rest of you bitches who just like a challenge—who can't appreciate

→

the worth of something until someone else has tried it on—shame on you. Here's another finger for ya.

roger dodger

A man who has lost (or never really found) the joy of sex, as a result of misogyny, insecurities, or his own heartbreak. Thus, he resorts to **phoning it in** or, worse, engages in **hate fucking** or **revenge sex**. Convinced that he's a master of **seduction**, a roger dodger is obsessed with increasing his **body count** as if to prove to the world what a stud he is (plus, it beats jerking off to **Internet** porn every night). From the 2002 movie *Roger Dodger*, starring Campbell Scott (the dude with the bad hair from *Singles*). A.k.a. a total douche bag. See also **ennui, cad, assholes**.

romance

What **casual sex** skeptics mourn the lack of in today's **hookup** culture. "Whatever happened to ritual, respect, roses?" they ask. But it's all a matter of perspective. Think of it this way: You're 22 years old, you're horny, you're drunk, you're **bi-curious**, and you're pretty damn sure you're a decade away from being marriage ready. You have no interest in long walks on the beach or Sunday-afternoon trips to Pottery Barn. You like **bars** and dancing and doing things that would shock your parents. Considering all this, traditionally romantic gestures would not only be inappropriate;

R

→

they'd be misleading. Why go through the motions of all that hand holding, just to keep up appearances? Why force yourself into **monogamy** when it just doesn't fit right now? Sure, some people prefer their sex with a liberal sprinkling of love (or something like it)—but, like your grandmother always said, there's more than one way to butter a slice of toast (though we're pretty sure she wasn't talking about the relative merits of a **booty call**). Besides, romance can pop up when you least expect it. Take our friend Saskia, who once promised herself that before she settled down, she wanted to try a **three-way** with two guys. She decided she'd do it while abroad, to give it an air of fantasy (besides, who wants to bump into their three-way compatriots while shopping for a plunger at the local hardware store?). So, one spring break in Cancun, she spied candidate A across the foam-filled dance floor of a club and introduced herself. Minutes later, they were playing tonsil hockey—

and, as they made out, she opened one eye to scope his friend, candidate B. "Want a **three-way**?" she asked. (Saskia has excellent **playdar**.) Emboldened by alcohol, sunstroke, and that foreign-land feeling that nothing really counts, they nodded in mute agreement. Candidate B was cocksure and completely at ease throughout the **sesh**, while candidate A was shy and hesitant. Saskia warmed to candidate A, and the following night she extended him a solo invitation. Fast-forward 3 years: Candidate A is Saskia's husband-to-be. They've composed an abridged version of the story for their parents and future grandchildren, but once every few months they'll laugh about that night, and about how it still feels like a fantasy—more of a **proxy** three-way than the real thing. Which just goes to show that a) you can never be sure that the first impression is also the last, and b) any story is romantic if it has a happy ending.

R

room of one's own, a

❶ A figurative term for one's mental/physical/emotional masturbation place. Have you self-loved today? No? Get back upstairs! You don't think Virginia Woolf was up there just *writing* all day, do you? ❷ Something that prompts the classic college pickup line: "Did I mention my roommate's out of town?"

rotation

A way of referring to one's coterie of **luvvas**, as in, "I just added Chad to my rotation. I'll probably have to give up my Bikram class to make room for him, but he's so worth it!" Heard almost exclusively on ABC's *The Bachelor*, as used by a candidate who announced that men frequently call her up to ask if they can "get in my rotation." Someone with a rotation—like, oh, say, that same candidate on *The Bachelor*—

may also announce, apropos of nothing, "Don't hate me because I'm beautiful." Don't hate us because we throw acid in your face, bitch.

rules, the

❶ A dating system devised by Ellen and Sherrie, the evil duo behind the best-selling *Rules* series of self-help schlock for women who want to land a man. If you're a woman and you don't want to be brazen, funny, or interesting, or have a good time (or good sex), or meet someone other than a big, fat, stupid meathead, by all means abide by Ellen and Sherrie's rules. Their books are full of wisdom on how "the average man" will react to "the average woman." Surely they intend *average* to mean the majority, but in the context of their advice and predictions, it comes to signify "boring, dull, mediocre." (And don't call us Shirley.) The authors employ some serious Cartesian logic to

→

get you to buy into their rules of engagement: "Don't ask why; just trust us," they say. "But why should we trust you?" we ask. Oh, right, we're not supposed to ask. They're a well-oiled propaganda machine with more fine print than a money-back-guaranteed five-day/25-pound weight-loss program. What, you didn't get a ring? You must have skipped Rule #625 ("Don't Break or Bend the Rules—Even a Little Bit"). Still haven't met Mr. Right? A Rules girl "does not get discouraged that there are no men out there and feel she must therefore bend the Rules to snag somebody. She trusts that the man of her dreams, whether offline or on, is out there and that all she has to do is follow the Rules and be patient." Perhaps it's pointless to criticize books for their blatant sexism when the authors admit to their sexism freely, loudly, obnoxiously, and as soon as page five. But we can't resist! "Equal rights and equal pay for women in the workplace cannot change a man's basic romantic nature."

Assumed differences in men's and women's "basic nature" were once used as a justification for women not being able to vote and work, too. This simplistic boys-will-be-boys mentality reflects the same kind of prejudice that keeps racism and homophobia going strong today. (By the way, equal pay across the board is still a goal, not a reality.) Ellen and Sherrie recommend that you "smile a lot" and "don't talk too much"— apparently, talking shows "nervousness and desperation and a bit of selfishness, since you're not allowing the other person to speak. . . . When you are married, you can talk to him every day, but hold back a bit for now." Ha! Send us a picture of him after the honeymoon, because we can't wait to see the look on his face when he realizes you are *nothing* like the woman he was engaged to. Oh, sure, Ellen and Sherrie have a dream: "Wow, did we wish we could just go to a party and talk to the really cute guy on the other side of the room, even if he didn't approach us.

→

R

We could wish all we want."
But we don't live in that kind of
world, damn it! Wait a minute—
yes, we do; it's the Rules girls
who don't. *We* can live by our
own standards and create new
realities; it's the Rules girls who
prefer to take the if-you-can't-
beat-'em-join-'em approach to
their personal lives. And, by
spreading this trend of status
quo relationship rituals, they
simply perpetuate a vicious
circle of stupid gender stereotypes. The Rules girls are the
devil! ❷ **Game playing**.
❸ Guidelines of behavior. The
only ones you should follow are
those outlined by us, the **team
player** at an **orgy**, the primary
in your **open relationship**, or
your **mom**.

R

S

sack record

Your track record when it comes to sex. See also **body count**, **stats**, **collectible**.

safe(r) sex

Reduced-risk rutting. The only truly *safe* sex is self-love (which includes, of course, mutual masturbation and **phoners**). But there is such a thing as saf*er* sex, and if you're hooking up, you better freakin' do your part. Seriously, folks, if you want to **play** in the booty sand-box, don't spoil it for the rest of us (and, while we're at it, don't pee in the pool, either). We may be dreamers, but we're realists, too: We know the timeline of a **one-night stand** does not allow for a visit to the **STD** clinic together. But you absolutely *must* use a **condom** and/or a dental dam. We don't care if

he's been your brother's best friend since kindergarten and swears he's been celibate since the Reagan years—it's just not worth the risk. If you like a sense of danger, do it with the blinds open. If you give a toss about your genitals, you should ask your bedmate what he or she is packing, as it were. Don't rely on someone to offer up details of their sexual history, no matter how pertinent these details may seem. There are men and women who walk (and shag) among us who figure that, hey, they're already infected with **HPV/herpes**, so if their one-night stand doesn't think to ask about it, why should they be the hero? Sadly, these men and women don't wear identifying name tags—in fact, they may appear to be perfectly sweet, kind, responsible, and **STD** free—so there's no way to guarantee you're not sleeping with one of them. Let's go over that one more time, shall we? There's no way to tell. His twig and berries may look immacu-late, she may volunteer for Planned Parenthood, he may

→

host bingo nights at the local old folks' home every Saturday night, she may go to church and blush at swearwords—all these people have the potential to withhold vital information about their sexual histories, or to not even *know* their own current sexual-health status. And, by the way, safer sex is a damn good reason to know who else is in your **booty call's rotation**. You may not care to be tied down by such old-fashioned principles as **monogamy**, but your nether regions tend to be a little more picky. Any kind of sex is a risk, but you deserve to know exactly what that risk looks like, especially since condoms don't protect you from everything (see **HPV** and **herpes**). On a final note: In case you'd forgotten, people lie to get laid. *All the time.* They lie about their job, their apartment, where they think they've seen you before, what they think about your eyes—and, yes, they lie about **STDs**, too. Sure, your partner of 5 years may cheat on you without a condom and lie about it, but

your one-night stand in Cancun is even *more* likely to lie to you. Hey, them's the stakes. It's why they call it saf*er* sex, after all. So, wrap the fuck up, already. (Isn't hooking up so much *fun*?!)

Samantha Jones

One of the four archetypal characters from *Sex and the City*: Samantha is the unapologetic **slut**, the queen of **casual sex**, the one who gets breast cancer as punishment from the gods for daring to enjoy a fuck for fuck's sake. She's independent, confident to a fault, financially successful, a **commitment-phobe**, superficial, selfish—you know, a *man,* except with gaudy jewelry and great tits (assuming the chemo worked). Samantha was played by Kim Cattrall, who till then was best known for her portrayal of the title character of the 1987 film noir classic

S

Mannequin, co-starring Andrew "Where Is He Now?" McCarthy. Cattrall tried to offset her ho-bag image with an earnest, heartfelt, feel-good sex manual co-written with her sensualist jazz-musician husband, Mark Levinson. *Satisfaction: The Art of Female Orgasm* promoted sexual exploration through deep love, commitment, and communication. A few months after *Satisfaction* was published in 2002, this loving, committed, and communicative couple realized they couldn't get no satisfaction and split up—and Cattrall decided to start playing the field like Samantha again.

sampler

A man or woman who subsists on a diet of sex and relationship "samplers." You know how some supermarkets offer tastings of new products in every aisle? If you're a cheapskate (and not a germaphobe), you can make a meal of it—melon squares in aisle 1, cheese and ham at the deli counter, brownies over in aisle 7. Keep doing laps, avoid making too much eye contact with the product reps, and sample away. In the world of hooking up, samplers ensure a balanced diet by relying heavily on **intimacy lite**. After all, nobody wants a steak for every meal, and nobody wants a hamburger every time, either—sometimes you just want to lie on the couch with a tube of Tums. That's a metaphor, folks.

Schrödinger's date

Something that feels kind of like a date but may be more

→

accurately described as a period of hanging out as a prelude to fucking. The term refers to the Schrödinger's cat application of the uncertainty principle: The date, like the cat, both is and is not. Among today's younger singles, **dating** has largely been superseded by the "Your place or mine?" **hookup** routine that's native to **bars** and clubs. In this world, you may be sleeping with someone on a regular basis but still not be quite sure whether you're actually **dating**. Shockingly, this highfalutin term originated with a bunch of nerdy Harvard students.

scope, to

To **cruise**, to be on the make, to keep your eyes peeled for **rec sex** opps, to play an adult game of I Spy (as in "I spy a **MILF** on a nearby park bench"). Usually uttered to one's **wing(wo)man** in public places where the **booze** is flowing, as part of the phrase "Let's scope the joint."

screen, to

To evaluate someone for their suitability for a position you have available: **one-night stand**, boyfriend/girlfriend, **booty call rotation**, etc. Candidates may be screened out based on a **Google** search (though beware the **Google-gänger**), a **dry run**, a **prenook** questionnaire, or a **reference check**.

Second Sex, The

Searing 1953 feminist tome by Simone de Beauvoir that famously begins, "Woman? Very simple, say the fanciers of simple formulas: She is a womb, an ovary; she is a female—this word is sufficient to define her. In the mouth of a man the epithet *female* has the sound of an insult, yet he is not ashamed of his animal nature; on the contrary, he is proud if someone says of him, 'He is a male!' The term *female* is derogatory not because it emphasizes woman's animality, but because it imprisons her in her sex, and if this sex seems to man to be contemptible and inimical even in harmless dumb animals, it is evidently because of the uneasy hostility stirred up in him by woman." Simone is, like, *such* a Miranda (see *Sex and the City*). See also **double standard**, *The Feminine Mystique*, **glass ceiling**, **virgin-whore complex**, **zipless fuck**.

seduction

The act of convincing someone to let you see them naked. May include any of the following: champagne and strawberries (see **sure thing**), surf and turf, poetry—correction: *good* poetry, a **primer**, flattering lighting, a neck massage, sweet nothings, sweets, sincere compliments, witty email repartee, karaoke. Contrary to popular belief, seduction should *not* include overdone R&B (see **soundtrack**), reading aloud from your manu-script, playing more than one song on your guitar (and one song only if you've been explicitly asked), shots of hard booze, Spanish fly, roses, Whitman's Samplers, dinner at the Olive Garden, Rohypnol, stalking. See also **catalyst**, **economies of scale**.

serial dater

Someone who tries on relationships like new outfits and handles breakups with éclat, occasionally shedding a single tear if it seems right. What if you like the kind of sex that comes with a monogamous relationship, but you aren't ready to settle down? You serial date. Serial daters like their **monogamy** in brief, intense bursts. They leave their baggage at home. They like long walks on the beach, but they're not particularly picky who's holding their hand by their side— it's just nice to have company, ya know? See also **romance**, **intimacy lite**.

sesh

Short for *session*: A meeting of two (or more) bodies for the purpose of transacting sexual business. There is (usually) no exchange of money, just pleasure. The term is used in the context of partners who have *regular* sex, whether as part of a long-term relationship, **appointment sex** you could set your watch to, **booty call**s with a reliable **friend with benefits**, or inappropriate visits with their therapist (as in, "I had a great sesh with my shrink yesterday. I had a real breakthrough—all over her face."). See also **facial**.

Sex and the City

❶ It was, like, this show on HBO—you might have seen it? It taught 13-year-old viewers that it's okay to talk about blow jobs at brunch (see **brunch story**). Beware the man who professes to like "the Charlotte type"—he Windexes the **glass ceiling** on a daily basis. If he likes **Samantha Jones**, he's either gay or he's at least 50, or he has fond memories of that 1987 movie *Mannequin*. If he's more of a Miranda type, it's probably because he heard that chicks dig guys who call themselves feminists, and he's trying to get into your pants. And if he says he prefers Carrie, it probably means he's never seen the show but thinks it might help him get laid if he pretends he has. As for those women who compare themselves to the show's characters (as in, "I'm totally a Carrie!" or "I'm, like, totally a contradiction: I'm part Charlotte and part **Samantha**!")— please don't make us go there. Can we all just agree to stop this insipid behavior? And, for the record, if a woman shows up to a **blind date** wearing her "I'm a Carrie" pink baby tee, you should feel free to break all protocol of polite behavior and walk away. ❷ The origin of some rather clever **hookup** lingo we wish we'd come up with ourselves, including **deja-fuck** and **toxic bachelor**.

Sex and the Single Girl

Helen Gurley Brown's best-selling 1962 guide to love, sex, and money. Gurley Brown was born in 1922 and didn't marry until she was 37 (which is, like, 103 in today's **dating** market); this book was her retort to the prim fifties manuals that, she said, "treated the single girl like a scarlet fever victim." Gurley Brown went on to edit *Cosmopolitan* magazine for 32 years; she used her editorship to encourage women to get on the Pill and then take *full* advantage of it. "Good girls go to heaven," she once said. "Bad girls go everywhere." Ah, remember the good ol' days, back when the Cosmo Girl stood for sexual liberation?

sex degrees of separation

A play on the term "six degrees of separation," behind which is the theory that anyone in the world is connected to everyone in the world by a maximum of six friends of friends. Replace the word *friends* with "**special friends**," and you get the idea. The concept is a key tool for sex educators trying to impress on their young students all the **STD** risks involved in sexual relations: Sleeping with someone is like sleeping with everyone *they've* ever slept with. The "six degrees" idea was first proposed by Hungarian writer Frigyes Karinthy in a 1929 short story called "Chains." Its most

recent pop-culture appearance was on Showtime's girl-on-girl drama, *The L Word*, in which one character creates a love-connection chart on her computer using a matrix program: "They're random acts of sex, 'k? They're encounters, romances, **one-night stands**, 20-year marriages. Anytime . . . you get a group of gay girls together, you are guaranteed someone slept with someone else. Who has slept with someone else, who slept with someone else, and on and on. Name any lesbian you know. I can link her to me in, like, six moves. So, the point is, we're all connected! See? Through love, through loneliness, through one tiny, lamentable lapse in judgment—all of us. In our isolation. We reach out! From the darkness! From the alienation of modern life. To form these connections."

Six Degrees of Separation was also a great play and an okay movie, both written by John Guare in the nineties and featuring gay male **casual sex** in a minor role. "Six degrees of Kevin Bacon" is another play on the term, which posits that every actor can be linked to the prolific *Tremors* star within six movies. Therefore, "sex degrees of Kevin Bacon" would be the theory that every actor who has done nude work on film can be linked to a scene featuring Kevin Bacon's naughty bits by six movies or less (see **equal opportunity objectification**).

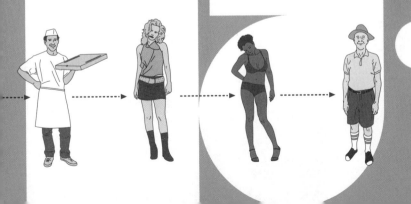

sexile

Someone who has been banished from their dorm room/apartment so that their roommate can get it on—as in "I've been sexiled tonight." College roommates (especially, though by no means exclusively, guys) will typically have a prearranged signal to indicate the act of sexile—perhaps a sock or a scrunchie on the door handle, or a note on the whiteboard reading, "I'm getting laid for the first time this semester, so don't you dare come in, fucker." Postcollege roommates tend to plan ahead for their periods of sexile, although **text messaged** sexile pleas after **last call** are not unheard of.

sexpat

Someone who travels to another (usually poor, Asian or Latin American) country for the sole (or near-sole) purpose of buying sexual favors from poor, malnourished, drug-addicted teens who were sold into the sex slave trade by their parents for twenty-five bucks. Capitalism at its best! A.k.a. sex tourist.

sexpectations

The sexual expectations that someone has of you, that you have of someone, or that you have of yourself. Though there are certainly reasonable expectations no civilized **rec sex** aficionado could argue with—like **prenooks**, decent **condoms**, **reciprocation**, clean sheets (at least, no *visible* stains)—there are plenty of others based solely on prejudice, stereotypes, and narrow-mindedness. Unreasonable sexpectations include: what worked on your

the eagle flies
at midnight

→

last partner will work on your new one; marriage is the death of hot, taboo-busting, throw-me-against-the-wall sex; if one partner doesn't climax, it's been a big waste of time; straight guys should not put things in their butts; mothers are asexual (see **MILF**, **virgin-whore complex**); and men should always do the asking out (and all the other beliefs held by **retrosexuals**). Then there are those sexpectations that gradually grow out of habits over long periods of time: You might think you have a "type," which keeps you from **dating** interesting brunettes, or maybe you believe you can't talk dirty in private because you never use swearwords in public. That's why **casual sex** is so appealing: It liberates you from those kinds of self-imposed sexpectations. But don't convince yourself that you need to go trolling for anonymous sex outside of your long-term relationship in order to feel liberated. Just spank your partner with a brand-new paddle after you've both marched in a peace rally

and see if that doesn't shake things up. See also **booty buzz**, **dress up**, **Halloween**.

sextra

❶ Something that exceeds your **sexpectations**, or a sexual **fringe benefit**. For instance, you sign up for a regular back massage and are pleasantly surprised with a **happy ending**. ❷ A **pinch hitter**. ❸ An extra in a porn flick.

signs

❶ Astrological symbols representing the twelve con-stellations in the zodiac that roughly correspond to the twelve months of the calendar. The sign you were born under helps determine the path of your life and your personality, and therefore can be used to determine your sexual compati-bility with other birth signs. And if you believe that, we've got some great real estate in Florida that we could sell you

→

at a rock bottom rate. **②** The focus of our weekly love-and-sex horoscopes on EmandLo.com, as told to us by a "real" astrologist. Hey, the kids seem to like it. **③** Part of a popular **pickup line** from the seventies: "What's your sign?" It didn't work then, and it certainly doesn't work now. See also **clichés**.

singleton

We have Bridget Jones to thank for this pejorative term for a single person; it is typically used only by a woman in reference to herself. A singleton is definitely not single by choice. She hooks up frequently and seems unable to grasp the fact that sucking dick is not the best way to tell a man you consider him **boyfriend material**. See also **smug marrieds**.

sloppy seconds (*nasty*)

① Sex with someone who's recently done it with a third party so that by the time you get there, things are a little, shall we say, *moist*. **②** Sleeping with a friend's recent ex. **③** Sleeping with someone who initially rejected your advancements in favor of a third party and came crawling back to you when things didn't work out with said third party. **④** A used sex toy.

slut

Noun: Someone who has more sex than you do. See also **body count**, **double standard**, **ethical slut**, **glass ceiling**, **reputation**.

slut, to

Verb: To have **casual sex**.

smug marrieds

A term, originally coined by Bridget Jones, for annoyingly self-satisfied couples who count their blessings in their wedded bliss, their cutesy joint tax returns, and their monogrammed bath towels. They act as if life were a race to find the One and they won (or at least placed), as if their matching wedding bands protect them from the kind of empty sex that all the pitiable **singletons** have, as if their marriage license guarantees them stability, security, and fidelity, as if participating in a wedding ceremony miraculously makes them mature, serious, worthwhile adults. Well, here's a news flash for you: Fifty percent of marriages end in divorce. Here's another: You *will* die alone, ball-and-chain beside you or not. Now, why don't you get the hell out of my face and go live happily ever after, fucktards.

snack, to

To make out at a **bar** or on the dance floor with no intention of getting **digits** or taking the person home or even **priming** them, because sometimes you feel like a nut, sometimes you don't. See also **I-can't-believe-it's-not-boinking**.

sober

*(No definition exists in the world of **casual sex**.)*

S

social circle

Your first degree of separation—i.e., the group of friends capable of introducing you to hundreds upon *hundreds* of "possibilities." Do we even need to explain why you shouldn't sleep with more than one person in your social circle at a time? In addition, if someone is in your social circle, you should start sleeping with that person only if you are prepared to go home with them (or go home solo) anytime you're hanging out with that person socially—i.e., you can't be on the same bowling team and go home with them after Wednesday practice but expect to sleep with the opposing team's captain after Saturday's tournament. Once this nebulous sleeping arrangement has been terminated, you may of course sleep with the opposing team's captain after a tournament game, though it probably won't do much for team morale. People, this is why it is a good idea to **slut** around *outside* your social circle. See also **sex degrees of separation**.

soundtrack

The music played in the background (or on an iPod with a double headset, à la *About Last Night*) during a seduction and/or a **sesh**. Contrary to popular belief, the R&B you danced to at a wedding does *not* make for sexy seduction tunes. Nor does smooth jazz or Enya, at least when it comes to **casual sex** (**anal sex** with a long-term partner is a whole 'nother story). Play anything from the online radio station Indie Pop Rocks for sex with skinny guitarists wearing wristbands, Billie Holiday or Elliott Smith

→

for **heartbreak sex**, Britney Spears for **revenge sex**, the Rolling Stones for **three-ways**, and the soundtrack to *The Last Temptation of Christ* for an **orgy**.

special friends

❶ **Friends with benefits**.
❷ **Luvvas** who started off as longtime friends. ❸ "**Just friends**."

speed dating

A kind of hypercaffeinated blind date marathon. Whoever said, "You can't hurry love" clearly has never experienced speed dating. In one evening (set up by a site like HurryDate. com), you get about thirty mini-dates, each lasting about 3 minutes. Sure, they're not the kind of dates where you share hopes, dreams, and your thoughts on God, but it's plenty long enough to decide whether you'd like to see each

other naked (just ask Malcolm Gladwell). Unfortunately, as anyone who played Two Minutes in the Closet in junior high will tell you, 3 minutes with the wrong person is a long-ass time. (Who invited the paste-eating kid to the basement party, anyway?) Fortunately, unlike junior-high make-out **seshes**, speed-dating events are highly organized: Hall monitors blow a whistle to let you know when your time is up, and no **digits** are exchanged on the spot—instead, you fill out a form with thirty yays or nays (no need to pick just one), and you're put in touch with each other only if the thumbs-up is mutual. Kiss those nasty **faux no.'s** good-bye!

speed dial

A number coded into your phone for rapid access to your **mom**, BFF, **booty call**, gyno, local Chinese take-out, or 1-900-IAM-EASY.

spouse swapping

It's a mini-**orgy** with a buddy system, when a round of Cranium (or sex with your spouse) just isn't cutting it anymore. Unlike in the case of **adultery**, everyone is in the know about who's fucking whom. In theory, that makes for very healthy, honest **casual sex**. But in practice? Well, don't expect to play Cranium again anytime soon with the couple in question—some things leave a mark that just can't be scrubbed out like so many red wine stains on your rug. A.k.a. wifeswapping (*archaic*), sleeping with the Joneses.

spring fever

If you're in a relationship, spring fever is that time of year when every person on the street seems more attractive, more underdressed, and more available than ever before. If you're single, it is that time of year when you fall in love once a day on the subway and find yourself **dry humping** the corner of your desk during lunch break. Spring fever is the perfect time to work on your **economies of scale**, become a **kissing bandit**, **snack** to your heart's content, expand your **rotation**, or dump the old ball-and-chain.

stats

❶ Your relationship status. ❷ Your measurements (either chest/waist/hips or length/girth). ❸ Your sexual history and health report. ❹ Your **body count**. ❺ Your **sack record**. ❻ All of the above.

STDs

Sexually transmitted diseases, or, the *huge* downside to **casual sex**. There are bacterial infections: chlamydia, gonorrhea, syphilis, bacterial vaginosis, chancroid, pelvic inflammatory disease (PID). There are parasitic infections: crabs, scabies, trichomoniasis. And there are viral infections: hepatitis, **herpes**, **HIV**, **HPV** and genital warts, molluscum contagiosum. (Other rarer ones certainly exist, but we can't spell them.) For the most part, if bacterial and parasitic infections are caught and treated quickly, they are curable and won't do permanent damage. Viral infections, on the other hand, have no cures; though some viruses may go away with a swift kick from a strong immune system, most tend to stick around for life (and may even cause the untimely end of that life). In all cases, some people may not show symptoms immediately or ever, so getting tested regularly is imperative, especially if you're having sex with multiple partners. Though porn, MTV videos, and romantic comedies ignore STDs like a kid with mild multiple sclerosis at the high school dance, infection and disease are a big reality of sex, whether casual or serious. You *must* use barrier protection if you really want to reduce your STD risks, but you also gotta know that a condom may not protect you from infections that are spread from skin to skin. Plus, if you're using some cheap, 10-year-old sheath and it breaks (or if you don't know how to use it correctly in the first place), you may be giving and/or getting the gifts that keep on giving. Along with condoms, regular testing (ideally together), good communication, and making sane/sober choices are all essential to reducing risk. Of course, those things don't usually go hand in hand with **rec sex**. In fact, some would argue that the whole point of **casual sex** is to live the fantasy by not talking too much and by getting

S

→

wasted to lower inhibitions. Well, those people are fuck-heads. See also **safe(r) sex**, **suspension of disbelief**.

STD ennui

The current backlash against those little red ribbons worn on lapels in the eighties and nineties, because fearing **casual sex** is, like, *so* last century. This attitude causes smart, well-educated, normally logical people to engage in incredibly *stoopid* behavior: **casual sex** without a **condom**. See also **safe(r) sex**.

Sting

Famous singer/songwriter with a longer shelf life than Madonna who sang about prostitutes and Lolitas as the front man of the Police, wore bikini briefs in the sci-fi flick *Dune*, played a hot Victorian Frankenstein with a necrophilia tendency in *The Bride*, writes love songs you want to hate but can't, is impossibly attractive even in his 50s (even to *hetero* dudes), and famously boasted he could make Tantric love to his wife for 8 hours. He even cleverly dug his way out of that doozy by later joking that he failed to mention that those 8 hours included 4 hours of begging and dinner and a movie. Oh, Sting. We constantly mock you, but only to mask our deep, unhealthy obsession with you, a god in human's clothes.

strike out

To not make it to any **bases** with a potential mate, probably because you used a lame **pickup line**, read your bad poetry out loud, or took a dump in their bathroom that they could smell from the next room.

strip poker/ Twister/ Scrabble, etc.

Pre-**orgy** favorites. See also **bull market**, **group sex**.

sugar daddy/ sugar mama

Someone who willingly funds a **gold digger** because they have more money than God—and, really, what's a few thousand dollars here and there if a sweet young thing a few decades your junior is willing to suck your toes, among other protrusions? A potential sugar daddy or sugar mama will not bat an eyelid when you order the most expensive thing on the menu and don't offer to go **dutch** (though men who react thusly may simply be **retrosexuals**). If you want a sugar parent of your own, don't go past first **base** until you've received a present of some kind. Make sure each date is exponentially more expensive, and hold out for an additional, exponentially expensive gift before passing each additional base. You wouldn't be so crass as to *request* these presents, but, like Skinner's rats, the sugar parent-in-training will begin to get the picture as they receive increasingly significant rewards. For example, you could suggest an afternoon date in your nearest chi-chi shopping district and see whether your companion offers to treat you to a new outfit when they catch you ogling it through the store window while

S

sighing about all your student loans. If, instead, they buy you *Personal Finance for Dummies*, we suggest moving on.

sure thing

Someone who is always good for a good time, à la Julia Roberts in *Pretty Woman*: When Richard Gere attempts to ply his hooker with champagne and strawberries, she tells him, "I appreciate this whole **seduction** thing you've got going on here, but let me give you a tip: I'm a sure thing." Or, why you don't need to arrange a candlelit bath for your **one-night stand**. Not that hooking is akin to hooking up, of *course*. But, people, we're all grown-ups here, and we all have "urges." Sometimes it's okay to simply give in to those urges without pretending that the night is about anything besides the sex.

suspension of disbelief

The willingness of **casual sex** partners to suspend their critical faculties to the extent of ignoring minor realities (a partner's annoying personality traits, their marital status, your marital status, the prevalence of **STDs**, the fact that you have to get up early for work, the fact that we're all boring human beings who eat and shit and do laundry very unromantically, etc.) so as to attempt to have sex like they do in the movies: passionately, acrobatically, and without consequence. A.k.a. living the dream. See also **sexpectations**, **zipless fuck**.

sweeps week

The last week of summer or spring semester, when everyone realizes they never got around to that fling they'd been planning on and makes a last-ditch

→

effort to rectify that sitch. If you can't get laid during sweeps week, then you're not really trying.

swinging

What happens when wild young things in **open relationships** grow up and amass lots of Tupperware but don't want to leave all that **free love** behind. Swingers are mostly heterosexual couples who mingle at house parties featuring mattresses in every room (and the occasional sex swing). Unlike **polyamory** enthusiasts, swinging couples reserve the romance for their spouses/life partners but share their bods unreservedly. The sex is social, casual, and often accompanied by passed hors d'oeuvres. F-on-F and M-on-F action is encouraged, though M-on-M action (a.k.a. sword fighting) is typically (and we'd say unfairly) frowned upon. Though they're usually suburban, the swingers in your neighborhood do not even remotely resemble the hotties on *Desperate Housewives*. But that doesn't stop them from basking in the cold, harsh light of the spotlight. (Witness HBO's *Real Sex* or the 1999 documentary *The Lifestyle*.) Swingers, bless them, never stop "exploring sex," and for that we salute them. Just close the blinds, please. See also **AdultFriendFinder.com**, **orgy**, **spouse swapping**, **three-way**.

S

T

take-me-back sex

Sex during a **closure** get-together, typically a few weeks to a month after a breakup. The initiator will show up for closure with a new outfit and a new gym body and fronting an I-love-my-new-life attitude. They will appear to accept all the terms of closure. And then, as the closure is coming to a close, they will oh-so-casually suggest a drink at the local **bar** "for old times' sake." Which leads to another, which leads to—*exactly*. The sex will be intense and fantastic, but their heart will break all over again when their partner reaches for a condom and sheepishly refers to their "recent activity." In the entire history of breakups and closure, take-me-back sex has worked exactly twice. Every other time, it ends in tears—a reopened breakup wound, a protracted **booty call** cycle, or another brief burst of **dating** before a second, even more painful breakup. Don't do it, petal. If you don't believe us, just ask your best friend—they've got our back on this one.

Tao of Steve, The

A movie about a slacker bachelor whose personal formula for getting laid is loosely based on Eastern philosophy: Rule #1: Be desireless. Rule #2: Be excellent. Rule #3: Be gone. It miraculously works—that is, of course, until Steve falls hard for a woman immune to his system, proving once and for all that there are no **rules** when it comes to tru wuv. The movie's got all the romantic comedy of a Julia Roberts vehicle combined with the indie cred of a Hal Hartley title, so it makes a great date rental, as long as you're not courting a **player** who will completely miss the moral of the story. See also **rules, the**.

team player

❶ The MVP of any group-sex setting, from a **three-way** to an **orgy**: They ensure that the CD never skips for more than a measure, that the chips and dip and bowls of condoms are constantly replenished, that everyone understands **the rules**, that no one is made to feel uncomfortable (all things being relative, of course), and that each attendee gets a little of what they came for. With a team player in the house, no one ever need feel like a third, fifth, or seventh wheel. ❷ A **pinch hitter**.

tease, a

A chronic flirt who never puts out: "Press against them when we dance / make them think they stand a chance / then refuse to see it through / that's the worst thing I could do." –Rizzo in *Grease.* See also **reputation**.

technical virgin

Assuming **virginity** is defined as never having had penile-vaginal penetrative sex, a technical virgin is any one of the following sexually active people: a gay man, a lesbian, a Catholic school student who has only **anal sex**, or a hetero woman who engages only in **outercourse** because she wants to wear white at her wedding (never mind the fact that she's guzzled more semen than Moby Dick). See also **loopholing**.

temp work

Casual sex you have until a better, more permanent relationship comes along. Thus, an overzealous matchmaking friend who likes to arrange **party favors**, an adult **online personals** site, an escort service, a brothel, or an Overeaters Anonymous conference could all be considered "temp agencies."

T

terror sex

As the country moves higher up the color-coded-alert warning system, the world of **casual sex** sees a ripple effect. As a general rule, for every level the country moves up, so the **bases** are shifted. For example, if you would normally give only a hand job on a first date during a Green period (low risk of terrorist attacks), you might upgrade that to **oral sex** during a Blue period (general risk of terrorist attacks) and to full-on boot knocking in a Yellow or Orange period. During a Red period (severe risk of terrorist attacks), expect **three-ways**, an **orgy** mania, and a significant rise in the national level of **bi-curiosity**. People who usually (i.e., during a Green or Blue period) feel it just isn't "right" to sleep around may (subconsciously) use a raised terror alert as an excuse to indulge— you're bonding, you're giving death the finger, you're celebrating life, you're living every day as if it were your last: "If we don't have a **one-night stand** tonight, the terrorists have won." A.k.a. doing it for your country, à la *Grease 2*. See also **occasion sex**.

text messages

Insta-communication for someone who hates their phone voice. Surely the text message was invented by a single man or woman in possession of a set of **digits** but too scared to make the call. Texting isn't just easy—it's sexy, too. By its very nature, texting is quick and dirty—so you can get away with "My place or yours?" and nothing else. Texting boils flirting down to its simplest form, encouraging anyone with a cellphone to embrace their inner dirty haiku writer. (Years of playing with erotic magnetic poetry have finally paid off!) Imagine this: Instead of stuttering an awkward message on someone's voicemail or trying to act nonchalant (while interested) on the phone, you can

→

use those digits to send a short, sweet, witty text message straight to their mobile device. Just as with an email, you can prepare ahead of time for maximum impact—but the limited space available means less chance of cracking a joke they'll take offense to. (Besides, who wants to ask the **bar** hottie for their email address? *So* dorky.) Plus, the very private can happen in public—call it exhibitionism for the shy. So texting, it seems, is the safest of all sex: no chance of **STDs**, unwanted pregnancy, or mood-killing embarrassment (first- or second-hand). Text messages are nonintrusive and yet instantaneous (because unless your booty call is hooked on their Crackberry, an after-hours booty email just won't do). A text message sent after midnight on a weekend or after 11 P.M. on a school night to your **umfriend** is known as a booty text—even if (or perhaps especially if) it innocently inquires, "Wot u up 2?" A.k.a. sexed messaging, sex messag-

ing, sext messaging, sexting. See also **appointment sex**, **booty call**, **bread-crumb trail**, **"I'll call you,"** **sexile**, **toothing**.

third-base coach

A new casual sex partner who is particularly vocal about giving specific direction and criticism (constructive or other-wise) during an early sexual encounter. As in, "Now move your finger to the right. No, that's too much, more to the left. Okay, steady now. That's it.

T

Get ready. Now go, go, go, go! Keep going!! All the way, you little bastard!!!" While honesty in horniness is to be applauded (see **quality control**), there is a fine line between offering supportive encouragement and micromanaging your fucking. Third-base coaches tend to cross that line.

three-way

Making the beast with six legs. We're sure there's a couple out there somewhere who have been going strong for 20 years and celebrate their anniversary each year by inviting a third party into the bedroom to make a human sex sandwich. Maybe they go out on the **pull** together and enjoy the tag-team flirting almost as much as the actual humping. Or perhaps they post an online personal together and spend the weeks leading up to their big day **screening** candidates. But let's be honest: Couples like that are rare (and probably strange) birds. They attend swingers' conferences in Vegas. We wouldn't be surprised if he's grown a long ponytail to compensate for a bit of balding on top, while she goes braless under her purple caftan. As for the rest of us, a three-way is much more likely to happen during a heavy **hookup** phase while at a party where cocaine or ecstasy is being imbibed. Three-ways are always awkward, but they're much *less* awkward if all three participants are a) single, b) strangers or mere acquaintances at the most—a decade-long secret crush is a no-no, c) comfortable with **casual sex**, d) **bi-curious**, and e) loaded (chemically or financially speaking). For the record, a three-way doesn't just mean two girls and a guy, despite what Hollywood and men's mags would have you think. Two boys and a girl works, too, you know—and, no, this doesn't have to mean porno-style double penetration: Don't you remember how to take turns? And boys, agreeing to an MMF three-way doesn't make you gay or even bi-curious; it just means you're open minded, eager to fulfill a girl's fantasy, and our hero. A.k.a. threesome. See also **ménage à trois**, **romance**.

timing

Apparently, it's everything. At least when it comes to good fortune in love and sex. For instance, *good* timing is being dumped the day before you run into your old high school sweetheart, who looks *amazing*, at which point you two go to dinner, catch up over drinks to find you're still the same people you were 20 years ago, then, while walking home, buy a lottery ticket together using the numbers of both your birthdays, and once home fuck like teenagers (that's a good thing). The next day your lottery number hits, and you move into a mansion together, get married, have beautiful babies, and live happily ever after. *Bad* timing is prematurely ejaculating on your partner's leg as your mom walks in to announce that Thanksgiving dinner's ready.

TiVo

A digital video recorder (DVR) that allows you to live by the ideal that television should never take priority over sex. It's right up there with the **Internet** and the **Rejection Hotline** as one of the greatest inventions of the past few years. Let's say you're watching the season finale of *The Amazing Race*, when the limbo competition makes you and your partner randy (it's okay—we *understand*): Just hit Record, abscond to the bedroom for some hot monkey love, and return 10 minutes later to pick up right where you left off. Plus, now you can breeze through the commercials! Life is good. See also *Daily Show* **factor, the**.

T

tofu boyfriend/ tofu girlfriend

Someone you go out with because they go with everything (see **arm candy**) or because you can bend them to your will and they will take on your flavor (see **Method dating**).

toothing

Finding a (usually anonymous) sex partner using a Bluetooth-enabled device (cell phone, etc.). One can transmit **text messages** to nearby devices in the hopes that someone will take the bait and agree to **hook up** in the nearest dark corner, public bathroom, or dive motel. Best for impatient perverts who consider posting an ad on **Craigslist** at 10 A.M. offering lunchtime nookie "*delayed* gratification." See also **cruising**.

toxic bachelor

Sex and the City synonym for a **cad** or **commitment-phobe**. Like **cadettes**, toxic bachelorettes are rarely sighted in the wild. See also **assholes**, **ladies' man**, **playa**, **player**, **roger dodger**.

toys

Great accessories for a night of **rec sex** (as long as they're not of the BDSM variety or previously soiled). Please see *Em & Lo's Sex Toy: An A-Z Guide to Bedside Accessories* for an entire book on the topic!

T

trisexual

When you can't decide which you like best: sex with boys, sex with girls, or sex with yourself.

try-sexual

Someone who's just like **Mikey**! You'll try anything–*once*. In fact, half the time we think you might be doing something solely for the brag value of having tried it. Maybe you should stop trying so hard and start figuring out what you actually enjoy. See also **collectible**, **doing it for science**.

U

a little sadistic in the sack (biting, hair pulling, name calling, etc.). Just don't break out the **handcuffs**.

u-were-wrong-to-leave-me sex

It's what **take-me-back sex** is called when it's initiated by a cynic or a realist (or someone who's read this book). You know it's never going to work, but you just can't help yourself, and you figure, hey, the odds of your ex coming to the postcoital realization that they were wrong to leave you are slightly better than those of you winning the state lottery. At the very least, maybe you can make your ex rue the breakup just a little. U-were-wrong-to-leave-me sex is more acrobatic and less about deep eye contact than take-me-back-sex—the intent being to impress rather than to bond. If you're the initiator, we bet you'll be on top, and we wouldn't be surprised if you got

umfriend

An acquaintance of nebulous status, as in, "This is my . . . um . . . friend." Your companion may suddenly downgrade you from new girlfriend/boyfriend status to an umfriend when they unexpectedly bump into a recent ex who is either heartbroken-slash-psycho or someone your companion would like to get back together with (sorry, sucker).

uncut

To have an uncircumcised penis—and we don't point and laugh at these anymore, kids. Circumcision is no longer routine in hospitals, so don't be surprised if you start seeing a lot more hooded warriors in your hookup travels (assuming

→

that penises, in general, are on your itinerary). The jury's still out on which way is better—some claim that the turtle-necks have sensitivity on their side, while others say that crew-necks are more hygienic. But really, once it's hard, what's the diff? Hooded handjobs may not require lube—ask the penis owner what he prefers. Turtle shell or not, if it's going inside any body cavity, slap a condom on it and proceed as usual. A.k.a. pig in a blanket.

under the influence

To be so affected by **booze**/perfume/pheromones/lust/desperation/hypnotism/beauty/fame that your inhibitions are dramatically lowered or your judgment severely impaired. For example, let's say you make it backstage at a Limp Bizkit concert: Offering up your bare ass as a target for the band's game of Toss the Cold Cuts may seem like a really good idea at the time, simply because you're intoxicated by their celebrity (not to mention all those whippets you did before the show). Sweetpeas, it's a *terrible* idea.

understudy

The less-than-desirable person who suddenly becomes the leading man/leading lady in a **wing(wo)man** bait and switch. There you are, being chatted up by a *total* fox, and the only thing on your mind (besides the obvious) is that you must remember to **text message** your roommate with a **sexile** request for the night. And then, those seven deadly words: "Hey, have you met my friend Pat?" Except what they really should have said is, "Hey, have you met my much uglier/shorter/hairier/drunker/duller friend Pat?" Yep, you have just been slipped an understudy. Enjoy your last view of that hottie's ass as they walk away to leave you and Pat to "get to know each other."

unicorn

❶ Any creature that is considered to be rare—or even mythical—in the world of **rec sex** and **dating**. For example, a single, straight guy with a sense of humor, a sense of style, and no commitment issues; a sexy, confident woman who really means it when she says she prefers nice guys; a sexy, confident woman who really means it when she says she's not looking for a relationship; a female model who can count past ten without using her toes; a male model who really means it when he says he's straight. Of course, some people would say that the only way for these unicorns to exist is if you truly believe in them. And that's one to grow on. ❷ A person wearing a strap-on dildo on their forehead.

unilateral casual sex

Having sex in a vacuum. No, we don't mean sticking your dick or your clit in the end of a Hoover (bad idea, by the way). We mean fucking as if there's no one else involved in the process. And, no, we don't mean masturbating (*always* a good idea). We mean having sex with someone without consideration for their feelings, their safety, or their pleasure. For example, it's just sex to you, but you know your bedmate thinks it's the beginning of a beautiful relationship—and you allow them to continue thinking this. Or they give you an orgasm but you don't even *try* to return the favor. Or you feel a **herpes** tingle on your lip but go down on your partner without a dental dam anyway. A.k.a. using someone, heinous. Antonym: **prenook**. See also **reciprocation**.

unrequited lust

What masturbatory fantasies are made of.

urban tribe

Term coined by author Ethan Watters because he was tired of explaining to his parents why he was over 30 and neither married nor producing off-spring. An urban tribe is a community of postcollege singles who act as an extended family and provide the kind of support you'd otherwise get from a long-term partner. In other words, your drinking buddies (but *you* didn't think to give it a catchy name and write a book about it, did you?). Your urban tribe is there for you on major holidays like T-Day and V-Day (not to mention during the Sunday-night blues) to ward off any seasonal **ennui** you may be suffering—no **smug marrieds** allowed. A member of an urban tribe isn't opposed to marriage and/or breeding in principle—they're just not there yet (so please, Mom, stop trying to set me up with your dental hygienist). See also **quirkyalone**.

V

vanilla

A vanilla sex life is a strict diet of bland, uninspired, missionary-position* sex—the kind your parents have (unless they own a copy of *The Joy of Sex* or they borrowed your copy of *The Big Bang*). There's no place for such boring boffing when it comes to **casual sex**. Actually, there's no excuse for boring boffing anytime, anywhere, anyhow—unless you have a broken leg or are over eighty.

*We're not against the missionary position in principle—it can be quite exciting, in fact. But it does tend to be the favored position of vanilla luvvas. Missionary, like tofu, means adding your own spice, whereas doggy style feels dirty no matter how dull you feel.

virgin-whore complex

A psychological/philosophical syndrome wherein a man (or a self-hating woman) puts females into one of two mutually exclusive categories: respectable, non-sexual, virginal mother (Jesus' mommy, Mary) *or* totally hot but sinful **slut** (Jesus' "**special friend**," Mary Magdalene). A man with **double standards** who likes the view down through the **glass ceiling** may well mature into a boyfriend or husband with a serious virgin-whore complex. He'll have learned to take hot **casual sex** for granted, having had many

→

happy affairs with many well-adjusted "**sluts**" over the years. But once he falls in love with a sexy, smart, beautiful woman, he'll start to wish that she could have acquired all those oral skills without all the practice. A.k.a. damned if you do, damned if you don't; Madonna-whore complex. See also **MILF**.

virginity

❶ The state of never having had sexual relations with another person, where "sexual relations" means you both got seriously naked and mutual pleasure was had. ❷ *Archaic*: Never having had penile-vaginal penetrative sex, which rather unimaginatively leaves out all the lesbians, gay men, and Monicas of the world. See also **technical virgin**.

W

walk of shame/ walk of fame

The return route to your own residence the morning after an unplanned sleepover, particularly after a formal-attire occasion when your prenoon tux or cocktail dress screams to passersby, "I got wasted last night and had sex with someone whose name I can't remember!" If you think that's a good thing and you're holding your head high and proud, it's a walk of fame. If you haven't been this embarrassed since that time in grade school when you accidentally shit your pants, it's a walk of shame.

"Was it good for you?"

If you have to ask, it wasn't. See also **clichés**.

Webmail address

It's a little pied-à-terre on the **Internet**! A Webmail address lets you correspond with someone without divulging your name, place of work, location, or even, really, your gender. Scoundrels use Webmail to conduct secret affairs, while the good people of the world simply rely on Hotmail to maintain a little privacy when dipping into **online personals** for the first time.

"What happens in [blank], stays in [blank]."

This motto is fitting after a drunken wedding/sober annulment in Vegas, a Jersey Shore **orgy**, or a spring break circle jerk. It is *not* appropriate if the groom sleeps with the "entertainment act" during his **bachelor party**.

"When will I see you again?"

Never, if you use crap **clichés** like that.

white lies

Little fibs that are acceptable at certain moments in life, though we generally frown on explicit and implied whoppers.

For example, if you've just broken his heart, does he really need to know you were lying all along about your feelings concerning the size of his dick? In addition, white lies may also be employed to answer the following questions: a) "Does my ass look big in this?" b) "Are you totally freaked out by the [fill-in-the-blank] fetish I just admitted to?" c) "Did your last boyfriend have a bigger dick than me?" As a general rule, if you can honestly say that the white lie you're telling is helping the person rather than just making your life easier, it's kosher. But if a white lie is simply postponing the truth because you can't face getting into all that right now, grow a spine. And, while we're on the topic, there wouldn't be such a need for little white lies if we could all agree to stop asking those questions that we don't really want honest answers to. (Not to be confused with that kick-ass Grandmaster Flash song about cocaine, "White Lines.")

wingman

❶ A hetero guy who'll brag about his hetero buddy in front of a female hottie so that Buddy gets to be all self-deprecating and funny while Hottie still gets to hear about Buddy's volunteer work/beach house/dot-com company/band/1600 SAT score. A wingman will flirt with all of Hottie's female friends, too (even if they're not so hottie) to make sure they don't leave en masse, taking Hottie with them. Finally, a wingman will convince the whole gang to move to a karaoke **bar** so Buddy and Hottie can bond over a duet performance of "Paradise by the Dashboard Light." (Note: Wingmen tend not to be effective devices for women on the make: Most guys will just assume he's your boyfriend.) **❷** A brilliant folk-song parody played over a Coors commercial that features the above scenario—in *slo-mo!*: "This chick's rockin' your bro on the dance floor. / But she's towing an anchor. / A junior investment banker. / Who's talkin' about herself and not much more. / Oh / So buy her a beer, / It's the reason you're here: / Mighty Wingman / You're taking one for the team, / so your buddy can live the dream: / Wingmaaaaaaaaaaaaan." **❸** A seemingly hetero buddy for whom you, a hetero dude, have homoerotic feelings, and with whom you may eventually have sex. Inspired by the hilarious Quentin Tarantino riff on *Top Gun* in the 1994 indie-flick *Sleep with Me*: "[*Top Gun*] is a story about a man's struggle with his own homosexuality. It is! That is what *Top Gun* is about, man. You've got Maverick, all right? He's on the edge, man. He's right on the fucking line, all right? And you've got Iceman, and all his crew. They're gay; they represent the gay man, all right? And they're saying, go, go the gay way, go the gay way. He could go both ways. Kelly McGillis, she's heterosexuality. She's saying, no, no, no, no, no, no, go the normal way, play by the rules, go the normal way. They're saying no, go the gay way, be the gay way, go for the gay way, all right? That is

→

what's going on throughout that whole movie. All right, but the *real* ending of the movie is when they fight the MiGs at the end, all right? Because he has passed over into the gay way. They are this gay fighting fucking force, all right? And they're beating the Russians; the gays are beating the Russians. And it's over, and they fucking land, and Iceman's been trying to get Maverick the entire time, and, finally, he's got him, all right? And what is the last fucking line that they have together? They're all hugging and kissing and happy with each other, and Ice comes up to Maverick, and he says, 'Man, you can ride my tail anytime!' And what does Maverick say? 'You can ride mine!' Sword fight! Sword fight! Fuckin' A, man!" Actually, the real line from *Top Gun* is, "You can be my *wingman* any time," but, really, same diff.

wingwoman

An improvement on the over-rated **wingman**. When a hetero woman sees a hetero guy hanging out with a bunch of cool chicas, she'll think a) he's a good laugh, b) he actually likes women, as opposed to just their body parts, c) he's not one of those desperate guys who plays video games every night and doesn't know how to talk to a woman if he's not trying to bed her, and d) he might actually respect her in the morning. Only really works when you have genuine female friends you can call on to help you work a club, and not when you have to hire female-friend surrogates from Wingwomen.com.

"Would you like to come in for a nightcap?"

A front-porch attempt to extend the festivities. You might as well say, "Would you like to come in for some hardcore animal fucking set to the musical stylings of Kenny G?" For a better approach, see **etchings**. See also **clichés**.

X

Xerox machine

The main reason to attend (or avoid) a **holiday office party**. We don't care if you *never* get around to a **three-way** or an **orgy** or a **booty call**—you haven't lived until you've photo-copied your naughty bits on the office machine. Do it once (and once is enough) before you settle down. Seriously, the office of the future won't even *have* a Xerox copier, so by the time you have grandkids, it'll just seem quaint. Your antique printouts might even be worth something on eBay someday.

Y

"Your place, or mine?"

Four words that automatically call to mind seventies swingers in polyester suits with mutton-chops and halitosis, thus making this phrase a quintessential **deal breaker**. See also **clichés**.

Z

zipless fuck

Guilt-free **casual sex** for women—imagine that! The term was coined by Erica Jong in her bestselling 1973 novel *Fear of Flying* (fifteen million copies in print and counting). Its married main character, Isadora, is "itchy for sex and itchy for the life of a recluse," "itchy for men, and itchy for solitude." So, what's a girl to do? "My response to all this was not (not yet) to have an affair and not (not yet) to hit the open road, but to evolve my fantasy of the Zipless Fuck. The zipless fuck was more than a fuck. It was a platonic ideal. Zipless because when you came together, zippers fell away like rose petals, underwear blew off in one breath like dandelion fluff. Tongues intertwined and turned liquid. Your whole soul flowed out through your tongue and into the mouth of your lover. For the true, ultimate zipless A-1 fuck, it was necessary that you never get to know the man very well. So another condition for the zipless fuck was brevity. And anonymity made it even better." Amen, sista.

Essential Reading

Essential Accessories/Tools

Essential Viewing

Essential "Social Networking"

Essential Safety

MY ROTATION

CODE NAME: ....   RATING: ☆ ☆ ☆ ☆ ☆

DIGITS: ....   EMAIL: ....

PREFERRED METHOD OF BEING REACHED: text / email / phone / drive-by

LATEST TIME TO CALL ON A WEEKNIGHT: ....

LATEST TIME TO CALL ON A WEEKEND: ....

FETISHES: ....

PET PEEVES: ....

LOCAL HAUNTS: ....

NOTES: ....

....

....

....

IN ROTATION? ....

CODE NAME: ....   RATING: ☆ ☆ ☆ ☆ ☆

DIGITS: ....   EMAIL: ....

PREFERRED METHOD OF BEING REACHED: text / email / phone / drive-by

LATEST TIME TO CALL ON A WEEKNIGHT: ....

LATEST TIME TO CALL ON A WEEKEND: ....

FETISHES: ....

PET PEEVES: ....

LOCAL HAUNTS: ....

NOTES: ....

....

....

....

IN ROTATION? ....

CODE NAME: . . . .   RATING: ☆ ☆ ☆ ☆ ☆

DIGITS: . . . .   EMAIL: . . . .

PREFERRED METHOD OF BEING REACHED: text / email / phone / drive-by

LATEST TIME TO CALL ON A WEEKNIGHT: . . . .

LATEST TIME TO CALL ON A WEEKEND: . . . .

FETISHES: . . . .

PET PEEVES: . . . .

LOCAL HAUNTS: . . . .

NOTES: . . . .

. . . .

. . . .

. . . .

. . . .

IN ROTATION? . . . .

CODE NAME: . . . .   RATING: ☆ ☆ ☆ ☆ ☆

DIGITS: . . . .   EMAIL: . . . .

PREFERRED METHOD OF BEING REACHED: text / email / phone / drive-by

LATEST TIME TO CALL ON A WEEKNIGHT: . . . .

LATEST TIME TO CALL ON A WEEKEND: . . . .

FETISHES: . . . .

PET PEEVES: . . . .

LOCAL HAUNTS: . . . .

NOTES: . . . .

. . . .

. . . .

. . . .

. . . .

IN ROTATION? . . . .

CODE NAME: .... RATING: ☆ ☆ ☆ ☆ ☆

DIGITS: .... EMAIL: ....

PREFERRED METHOD OF BEING REACHED: text / email / phone / drive-by

LATEST TIME TO CALL ON A WEEKNIGHT: ....

LATEST TIME TO CALL ON A WEEKEND: ....

FETISHES: ....

PET PEEVES: ....

LOCAL HAUNTS: ....

NOTES: ....

....

....

....

....

IN ROTATION? ....

CODE NAME: .... RATING: ☆ ☆ ☆ ☆ ☆

DIGITS: .... EMAIL: ....

PREFERRED METHOD OF BEING REACHED: text / email / phone / drive-by

LATEST TIME TO CALL ON A WEEKNIGHT: ....

LATEST TIME TO CALL ON A WEEKEND: ....

FETISHES: ....

PET PEEVES: ....

LOCAL HAUNTS: ....

NOTES: ....

....

....

....

....

IN ROTATION? ....

CODE NAME: . . . .   RATING: ☆ ☆ ☆ ☆ ☆

DIGITS: . . . .   EMAIL: . . . .

PREFERRED METHOD OF BEING REACHED: text / email / phone / drive-by

LATEST TIME TO CALL ON A WEEKNIGHT: . . . .

LATEST TIME TO CALL ON A WEEKEND: . . . .

FETISHES: . . . .

PET PEEVES: . . . .

LOCAL HAUNTS: . . . .

NOTES: . . . .

. . . .

. . . .

. . . .

IN ROTATION? . . . .

CODE NAME: . . . .   RATING: ☆ ☆ ☆ ☆ ☆

DIGITS: . . . .   EMAIL: . . . .

PREFERRED METHOD OF BEING REACHED: text / email / phone / drive-by

LATEST TIME TO CALL ON A WEEKNIGHT: . . . .

LATEST TIME TO CALL ON A WEEKEND: . . . .

FETISHES: . . . .

PET PEEVES: . . . .

LOCAL HAUNTS: . . . .

NOTES: . . . .

. . . .

. . . .

. . . .

IN ROTATION? . . . .

CODE NAME: .... RATING: ☆ ☆ ☆ ☆ ☆

DIGITS: .... EMAIL: ....

PREFERRED METHOD OF BEING REACHED: text / email / phone / drive-by

LATEST TIME TO CALL ON A WEEKNIGHT: ....

LATEST TIME TO CALL ON A WEEKEND: ....

FETISHES: ....

PET PEEVES: ....

LOCAL HAUNTS: ....

NOTES: ....

....

....

....

....

IN ROTATION? ....

CODE NAME: .... RATING: ☆ ☆ ☆ ☆ ☆

DIGITS: .... EMAIL: ....

PREFERRED METHOD OF BEING REACHED: text / email / phone / drive-by

LATEST TIME TO CALL ON A WEEKNIGHT: ....

LATEST TIME TO CALL ON A WEEKEND: ....

FETISHES: ....

PET PEEVES: ....

LOCAL HAUNTS: ....

NOTES: ....

....

....

....

....

IN ROTATION? ....

CODE NAME: . . . .   RATING: ☆ ☆ ☆ ☆ ☆

DIGITS: . . . .   EMAIL: . . . .

PREFERRED METHOD OF BEING REACHED: text / email / phone / drive-by

LATEST TIME TO CALL ON A WEEKNIGHT: . . . .

LATEST TIME TO CALL ON A WEEKEND: . . . .

FETISHES: . . . .

PET PEEVES: . . . .

LOCAL HAUNTS: . . . .

NOTES: . . . .

. . . .

. . . .

. . . .

. . . .

IN ROTATION? . . . .

CODE NAME: . . . .   RATING: ☆ ☆ ☆ ☆ ☆

DIGITS: . . . .   EMAIL: . . . .

PREFERRED METHOD OF BEING REACHED: text / email / phone / drive-by

LATEST TIME TO CALL ON A WEEKNIGHT: . . . .

LATEST TIME TO CALL ON A WEEKEND: . . . .

FETISHES: . . . .

PET PEEVES: . . . .

LOCAL HAUNTS: . . . .

NOTES: . . . .

. . . .

. . . .

. . . .

. . . .

IN ROTATION? . . . .

CODE NAME: .... RATING: ☆ ☆ ☆ ☆ ☆

DIGITS: .... EMAIL: ....

PREFERRED METHOD OF BEING REACHED: text / email / phone / drive-by

LATEST TIME TO CALL ON A WEEKNIGHT: ....

LATEST TIME TO CALL ON A WEEKEND: ....

FETISHES: ....

PET PEEVES: ....

LOCAL HAUNTS: ....

NOTES: ....

....

....

....

....

IN ROTATION? ....

CODE NAME: .... RATING: ☆ ☆ ☆ ☆ ☆

DIGITS: .... EMAIL: ....

PREFERRED METHOD OF BEING REACHED: text / email / phone / drive-by

LATEST TIME TO CALL ON A WEEKNIGHT: ....

LATEST TIME TO CALL ON A WEEKEND: ....

FETISHES: ....

PET PEEVES: ....

LOCAL HAUNTS: ....

NOTES: ....

....

....

....

....

IN ROTATION? ....